TRAVELLERS IN EIGHTEENTH-CENTURY ENGLAND

TEMPLE BAR, 1720
From an original etching by Cyril Barraud

TRAVELLERS IN EIGHTEENTH-CENTURY ENGLAND

by
ROSAMOND BAYNE-POWELL

BENJAMIN BLOM, INC.
Publishers New York 1972

First published London, 1951
Reissued 1972 by
Benjamin Blom, Inc.
New York, N.Y. 10025

Library of Congress
Catalog Card Number 74-174875

Printed in the
United States of America

CONTENTS

CHAP.		PAGE
	INTRODUCTION	ix
1	THE ARRIVAL—CUSTOM HOUSES	1
2	THE COACHES	8
3	ROADS, TOLLS AND HIGHWAYMEN	25
4	INNS, LODGINGS, COFFEE-HOUSES AND CLUBS	40
5	LONDON	55
6	AMUSEMENTS AND SPORTS	75
7	EDUCATION, ARTS AND THE UNIVERSITIES	92
8	THE POOR, HOSPITALS, CHARITIES	112
9	ENGLISH TOWNS	120
10	THE FOREIGNER IN THE COUNTRY	134
11	RELIGION, MORALS	154
12	THE FOREIGNER IN SOCIAL LIFE	168
13	FOREIGN QUACKS AND IMPOSTORS	189

LIST OF ILLUSTRATIONS

TEMPLE BAR, 1720 . . . . . *Frontispiece*
By courtesy of Messrs. W. F. Sedgwick, Ltd.

	Facing page
GRAVESEND FROM THE THAMES, 1773	2
EIGHTEENTH-CENTURY TRANSPORT BY ROAD	20
THE NEW INN, GLOUCESTER	44
LONDON FROM BLACKFRIARS BRIDGE	66
OXFORD (MAGDALEN COLLEGE; QUEEN'S COLLEGE AND THE HIGH	98
THE QUEEN'S HOUSE, ST. JAMES'S PARK	116
THE FOUNDLING HOSPITAL	116
BATH IN THE EIGHTEENTH CENTURY	126
HOLKHAM HALL, NORFOLK	140
ST. MARY'S IN THE STRAND, 1753	154
THE ROTUNDA, RANELAGH GARDENS, 1794	172
LEICESTER SQUARE	188

Introduction

From the days of the Ancient Britons there have been foreign travellers in England. The Phœnicians came here to trade in tin, during the Roman occupation there were visitors from the Continent, and there were other invaders, Jutes, Saxons, Danes and Northmen. Doubtless there were travellers who came in the wake of the conquerors, traders and others. There were the early Christian missionaries and later the itinerant friars. The Jewish money-lenders arrived and the Lombards from Italy, Flemish merchants who had heard of the excellence of English wool. There were even a few traders from the east. While communications were very difficult and travel dangerous few risked the journey to an island which was generally regarded as the land of barbarians, shrouded in impenetrable fogs and inhabited by a fierce, brutish people of uncivilized habits, who, it was said, ate raw meat and had no wine fit for a discerning palate. By the seventeenth century travel had become easier and less perilous. Englishmen had been seen on the Continent, who appeared to be quite tame and even moderately civilized. The Huguenots had found in Britain a happy asylum where they could worship unmolested, trade was increasing and, for one reason or another, the foreign traveller came in increasing numbers. In the early days of the eighteenth century there was quite an influx, as Englishmen noticed with disgust. Those Dutchmen whom William III brought over, or who followed him here, were not looked upon with favour. There was a blessed interval under Queen Anne when few foreigners came and then George I arrived, bringing with him a horde of Hanoverians, mistresses, place-hunters and servants. They were all rapacious, the Englishman declared; they all wanted to batten on the country; the King's mistresses were old and ugly and the monarch only spoke German and had unbecoming ideas about economy. On the heels of this horde of courtiers and hangers-on came a crowd of hungry Germans, some of whom settled in and upon the country. Others arrived to stay with their relatives or to travel about England. By the end of the century it was computed that 30,000 Germans were living in London.

England was, in fact, a sort of El Dorado, "That land whose very name is music in our German ears" as one enthusiastic traveller termed it. Here they had more liberty than in their own countries—indeed most travellers, whether they were Germans, French, Swiss or Portuguese, harped upon the blessings of English liberty; the standard of living was, on the whole, higher than on the Continent and the mass of the people were better off. The French republican traveller Meister thought, indeed, that they were too well off. "Why" he demands " is the soil of England so well cultivated ? It is because England is rich." "Why is England the seat of liberty ? It is because England is rich."

"Why does England, at present, pay so little regard to the attainments of art and literature ? It is because England is too rich."

"Why is not England more peaceable and happy ? It is because England is too rich. Gold is the sun of the nation."

Whether men were attracted by this sun and came to bask in it and trade, or whether they came to visit relations, or as mere tourists, there is no doubt that a steady flow of foreigners came into this country during the century. They saw England from many angles, they were biased by their education and their preconceived ideas. Some of them, like Sophie de la Roche, gushed over its merits and beauties and excused the coarseness of manners on the plea that it was essentially English, others like von Uffenbach could see very little that was good in the people or the country and were glad to leave it.

In this book it is proposed to give some account of what the foreigner saw in England, how he travelled and was entertained, whether he liked his hosts, and what they thought of him, and his various reactions to what he saw and experienced.

CHAPTER I

The Arrival—Custom Houses

THE traveller who arrived upon our shores had often spent days or even weeks upon his journey. He had perhaps travelled long distances by coach or diligence to the port of embarkation. There he had often spent tedious hours waiting for the wind to rise, to change, or to abate. He had set sail in small miserable ships, having, as a rule, to bring his food with him. He had probably suffered the miseries of sea-sickness, he may have been bruised and battered by storms; often he arrived in a disgruntled frame of mind, ready to find fault with everything. It is surprising indeed that any foreign traveller saw, in these circumstances, anything to admire. Travellers could cross from Calais to Dover, Dieppe to Brighthelmstone, Rotterdam to London, Ritzbuttel to Yarmouth. Much of the conversation among them—if indeed they were in any condition to talk—would have been about the customs, and the chances of evading them. As the shores of England loomed in sight, little boats slipped furtively from the coast, and approaching the ship, their crews offered to transport anything that was dutiable and restore it safely and secretly when the owners were in England. Naval frigates and corvettes might, upon occasion, offer this service. The travellers would have been in a difficulty. Did they dare accept? The men in the boats looked a rascally crew and were almost certainly smugglers, the

THE ARRIVAL—CUSTOM HOUSES

sailors of His Majesty's navy looked even worse. No man, Dr. Johnson had said, would go to sea in a King's ship who could contrive to get himself into a jail. It might be better to keep their dutiable articles and try what a little bribery would do, or if the worst came to the worst, to pay duty upon them.

The most horrible journey comes miserably to an end and at last the weary traveller saw the white cliffs of Dover or Brighthelmstone, the Yarmouth lighthouses or the Thames at London docks. They were pitching and tossing, waiting for the boats which were rowing out and which would take them to the shore. It was not always a pleasant prospect which was spread before them. There were poor, mean houses, noisy, jostling crowds, sailors fighting in a ring with their backers egging them on, the stench which arose from ships in harbour, a crowd of bawds, pimps and pickpockets waiting to prey upon the foreigner. No wonder that the German colony in London kept a watch at the docks to guide any countrymen who arrived through cut-throats and custom houses. Bribery was universal. Pastor Moritz, that good, German clergyman, who, it might be thought, would have had a few scruples, paid six shillings to get his luggage unexamined through the Dartford customs He only regretted that the transaction had cost him so much. Count Kielmansegg tells us that his pockets as well as his clothes were searched at Harwich, and as he arrived after nightfall he had to leave his luggage in the charge of his servants to be examined by daylight. " It is possible " he said " with the aid of a guinea or so to avoid too strict an examination, if the officers are assured that the things are for your own use."

Mme de Bocage, after a most miserable crossing from Calais, was told by the pilot of the ship she was in that it was impossible, owing to the high seas, to enter Dover

GRAVESEND FROM THE THAMES, 1773

harbour. He suggested that she should get on board a small vessel which would take her and her husband to Deal. Poor Mme de Bocage, who had given up all hope of ever seeing her family and friends again, or even seeing England, accepted what she called "that sad proposal". "The captain" she continues "took me into his arms to help me into the boat, which the waves constantly drove from the vessel, so that a slip which he made upon the ladder obliged him to let go: by good luck instead of falling into the water, I found myself alone upon this skiff in the midst of the rowers, at the mercy of the waves and trembling with fear lest M. de Bocage should not be able to come to me." Eventually she and her husband reached the shore, and the custom house. Hastily they declared everything, paid everything, cursed everyone and set out to find lodgings. Mme de Bocage describes these as wretched, but confesses that they were better than anything which could be found in France in a similar place.

Von Uffenbach got his luggage through the Harwich customs without any bribery. The officials " stared hard" he tells us " at twelve new shirts I had bought in Holland; however, as they had my name, and were purposely tumbled, they were allowed to pass." He set out hopefully on his journey to London; but when he had gone twelve miles and reached Manningtree, he was stopped and all his luggage was to be examined again. He found that this time it was only in order to extract a "trinkgeld" and, when this was disbursed, he was allowed to proceed without opening his boxes. In London they were searched again; but with what results he does not say. Ships arriving at a port were also examined. De Saussure tells us how five or six separate parties of officials boarded his vessel at Gravesend, to each of whom the captain made a present: " for ships" de Saussure says " are occasionally much damaged by these visits, the searchers being allowed to break down the wooden partitions so as to make sure nothing is concealed in them, and the more generous the captain shows himself the less harm is done to the ship. Some pounds of tea were found, hidden away between the stones of the kitchen stove of our vessel." When they reached London there was another search. A French refugee captain excited suspicion as being " rather bulky in the seat" and a packet of Flanders lace was found concealed in his breeches. He was accompanied by his mother and sister and " the customs men were impudent enough" de Saussure says "to search beneath the French lady's petticoats". The hooped petticoat had been known to conceal a man, and was a capacious hiding place for contraband. "They did not draw their hands out empty" de Saussure continues, "but produced several more packets of lace."

It seems strange that in an age when so much beautiful English lace was made, it should have been lucrative to smuggle in Flemish lace; but as far as dress was concerned, and perhaps only in that particular, English women were convinced that foreign goods were better than English.

Casanova, we are not surprised to learn, had difficulty with the custom house. " English officials" he complains " cannot be compared to the French, who know how to combine politeness with the exercise of their rights." Travellers have often complained of the attitude of these officials; but it was not only the customhouse men who were rude to foreigners. England was, in those days, extremely parochial. Anyone outside his own town or village was considered by the native to be a foreigner, and the man who came from that outlandish place the continent of Europe was a strange being, who ate frogs and snails, disliked good English beer and had not the advantage of being an Englishman. " I do not think " de Saussure says " there is a people more prejudiced in its own favour than the British people and they allow this to appear in their talk and manners." There were instances of foreigners being insulted and even attacked by the London mob; but as a rule they were regarded with a hearty contempt, and most foreigners speak of being received with a rather frigid politeness, and even, on occasion, with great consideration.

" They are generally polite people " says Zetzner who came from Strasbourg in 1700 and stayed two years in this country, " with a developed political intelligence, clever and of a fine stature. They have a remarkably penetrating mind, learning and understanding everything. They are also agile, muscular, good at all bodily exercises. They can be kind, and if they wish to do honour to someone, they spare no pains. But in the depth of their soul they are proud, haughty and they consider themselves superior to other nations. The kindly Moritz, who suffered so much at the hands of innkeepers, says that " the English were taxed, perhaps too hastily with being shy and distant to strangers. I do not think this was ever formerly their character." Some travellers are extravagant in their praise. " Even the tax gatherers are honest! " a Frenchman exclaims. " These people " declares Meister " are honourably distinguished by sentiments of decorum, magnanimity and uprightness, by private attachments and universal benevolence, by affections of every gentle, constant and generous kind, which the heart is capable of feeling." It is pleasant, in this age when our country is being generally abused, to read such a tribute.

The Englishman, however, was not easy to know, and

the first impressions of our country were generally far from favourable. " St. Catherine's (Dock) is one of the most execrable holes in all this great city " says Moritz. " He who lands here first sees this miserable narrow dirty street and this mass of ill-built, old, ruinous houses, and, of course, forms at first sight, no very favourable idea of this beautiful and renowned city."

" This beautiful and renowned city " had probably some of the worst slums in Europe. Its population had immensely increased during the century. At the beginning of our period, it was probably about half a million, and by the end had swollen to 750,000. Zetzner, who lived for some time with a London merchant and dealt with his foreign correspondence computed that there were 120,000 houses, 5,000 streets, 140 churches with bells and 960,000 inhabitants; but as there had never been a proper census it is impossible to assess the population correctly.

A great increase in building was noticeable. Archenhotz declared that 43,000 houses had been built in ten years; but the houses erected were chiefly for the upper and middle classes. The poor were herded together in a state of unimaginable squalor and gross over-crowding. Some of the worst slums were in the neighbourhood of the London docks, and they were peopled, for the most part, by thieves, cut-throats, prostitutes and pimps. Meister the Frenchman, who visited England in 1789 and again in 1792, says of this part of London. " Both banks of this delightful river are covered with the most filthy erections, old stables or the miserable huts of fishermen and watermen ... the inhabitants are shut out from the richest prospect which the happy situation of that capital is capable of affording them." He was probably comparing it very unfavourably with Paris, whose river was not shut out of sight by wharves and slums.

If the traveller arrived in London by road, he would have been gratified by the sight of pleasant, suburban houses set in gardens. These were the residences of London citizens, their little boxes as they called them where they often lived or sometimes used as weekend resorts. Macky writes of the two hundred little country houses which had been built at Wanstead " for the conveniency of the citizens in the summer, where their wives and children generally keep, and their husbands come down Saturdays and return Mondays ". The slums, however, had begun to invade the country. Squalid houses were being built close to the citizens' pleasant dwellings. Even those " South Sea " seats which Macky speaks of, the abode of those fortunate men whom the Bubble had enriched, had some very unpleasant neighbours. Heaps of cinders, filth and ordure from the great city were collected outside it, some of which went to manure the market gardens, but much remained to pollute the atmosphere. London and other large towns could be smelt as the coach approached it on the country roads. Grosley tells us of houses, built one brick thick and that made " of the first earth that comes to hand and only just warmed at the fire . . . the inside of these buildings " he adds " is as much neglected as the outside, small pieces of deal supply the place of beams, all the wainscoting is of deal, and the thinnest that can be found."

At last, however, the foreign traveller, whether he arrived by ship, by coach or posting in his own carriage, was set down at his inn or lodging, tired certainly, disgusted and disgruntled probably and seldom able to echo the panegyric of one enthusiast who exclaimed on arrival :

" The mere thought this is England made me leap for joy and bless the land of that noble friendship which had prepared such unspeakable pleasure for me."

CHAPTER 2

The Coaches

ONCE having reached an English port, the aim of all travellers was to leave it as soon as possible. There were several means available. English people of the upper classes generally travelled in their carriages, drawn by their own horses, or when posting had been established, by post horses. A wealthy foreigner sometimes adopted this form of travel. Count Kielmansegg hired a landau and horses in London, for a tour through England. For this he had to pay 27*s*. a day; but before they got to Oxford the roads had become so bad that the coachman insisted on turning back. The count being a foreigner and unable to cope with recalcitrant Englishmen, meekly hired two post-chaises, and made his way with his party to the University City, his servants riding on behind him.

Sophie de la Roche, a German in spite of her name, had a pleasanter experience. She hired, also in London, " a pretty carriage for three drawn by two horses and a friendly coachman " for 15*s*. a day; but then nothing tiresome ever seemed to happen to Sophie. She was full of the praises of England, and no one apparently had the heart to disappoint her.

This method of travelling was not usually adopted by those who had just arrived from the Continent. It was very expensive and required a fuller knowledge of

English, and of current coaching slang than the newcomers generally possessed.

The hardy Englishman frequently travelled on horseback. It was a pleasant and independent way of going in summer and if the weather were good. Bad roads and miry patches could often be avoided by taking cuts across fields or over heaths, one saw the country at one's leisure and saved the money for coach hire. On the other hand a man riding alone was liable to be attacked by highwaymen. He must know the language and the roads or he might go far out of his way and find himself benighted in a bog. He would be obliged to send all the property, which he could not cram into two saddlebags, by the stage waggon or by sea, with the risk of never seeing it again. "The English traveller on horseback" says Meister "displays an extraordinary degree of resolution. We see more wooden legs here than in any other country." This was possibly an aspersion on English horsemanship. Owing to bad roads and furious driving there were probably more accidents to coaches and post-chaises than to riders on horseback.

Be that as it may, the foreigner arriving at an English port, generally looked around for some other method of transport. Perhaps he consulted the landlord, and if he were staying at a really first-class inn, which catered only for the quality, his host would assure him that no gentleman travelled except by post-chaise. This method of conveyance became common about the middle of the century. The chaise usually held two persons, with a dicky behind for the servants; it was lighter than the old lumbering coaches and went at a faster pace. There was no coachman and the horses were driven by a postboy who rode on one of them. These post-boys were usually grown men, some of whom were quite elderly and had been in that employment for years. Theirs was a hard life, exposed to wind and weather, contending with bad roads, tired horses and the vagaries and stinginess of passengers. No wonder that there were many complaints about them, that they were often surly, frequently drunken and sometimes in league with the highwaymen who infested the roads. These bandits would often have post-boys in their pay, and if a particularly wealthy-looking guest was leaving the Angel or the George, word would be sent by an underling of the stable that a gentleman worthy of their attention would be travelling up the London road at such and such an hour on the following day.

The post-boys generally wore a uniform, perhaps of green with gold braid and a cocked hat, though Moritz speaks of the one he had, who " wore his hair cut short, a round hat and a brown jacket of tolerable fine cloth with a nosegay in his bosom ". They expected to be given a tip of 3d. a mile. This, with the 1s. 6d. a mile charged for posting and 6d. to the ostler when the horses were changed, made such a mode of travelling very expensive. Indeed when we consider the value of money, and that prices have risen enormously for most commodities during the last 200 years, we may conclude that a journey was then about the most expensive thing a man could undertake.

The stage-coach was certainly cheaper. The charge was 2d. or 3d. a mile with tips at the end of the journey to guard and coachman. In his own country the foreign traveller had been accustomed to the stage-coach or diligence and it was by this means that he usually journeyed to his destination.

The stage-coaches were heavy, lumbering vehicles. In the earlier days of the century they were generally covered with dull black leather, studded with nails, the frames and wheels being picked out with red. The windows were then covered with boards or sometimes with leather curtains. Pastor Moritz, who came to England in 1782, found a coach of this description still upon the roads, and having a taste for fresh air and sunshine he complained of a fellow traveller, a farmer " who seemed anxious to shun the light and so shut up every window he could come at ".

It was not the light to which the farmer objected— no one in England minded light, but they did most strongly object to the air which came through a window. This, as was well known, was most prejudicial to health and nearly everyone would have agreed with Mr. Woodhouse on that subject.

The coaches of the early eighteenth century were entirely devoid of springs. They lumbered along at four miles an hour or even less, drawn by three horses, " unicorn " as it was called, and a post-boy sat on one of the pair.

Misson, a French traveller who visited England in 1719, tells us of " the coaches that go to all the great towns by moderate journeys, and others which they call flying-coaches that will travel twenty leagues or more; but these do not go to all places ". At that date these flying-coaches were not common, nor was their speed in any way excessive.

The old stage-coaches were certainly better than anything of their kind to be found on the Continent. " These " quoting Pastor Moritz again " are at least in the eyes of a foreigner, quite elegant, lined in the inside and with two seats, large enough to accommodate six persons; though it must be owned when the carriage is full the company are rather crowded." He was to find one stage-coach that had twelve to fifteen people on the top. This crowding of the coaches was a common complaint. They were built to carry four passengers in comfort inside and not more than six were supposed to ride on the top. Then there was the basket or rumble-tumble. This was described in an advertisement in the *London Evening Post* of 1751 as "a conveniency behind the coach for luggage and outside passengers". We may see this basket with an old woman sitting in it in Hogarth's picture of the *Inn Yard*. Poor Pastor Moritz did not find it a conveniency. Tired of crouching on the curved roof of the coach, hanging on to a small, wooden handle, he prepared to slip down into the basket. "A blackamoor", his fellow-passenger, tried to dissuade him, pointing out that he would be half killed; but he was so uncomfortable where he was that he resolved to risk it. At first, as they were going uphill, he was fairly comfortable, indeed he was nearly asleep, when the coach began to go downhill and all the bags and parcels fell upon him. He was so much bruised and shaken that he was glad to climb back to insecurity on the roof. "The getting up there alone" he said "was at the risk of one's life" and yet, he tells us, women sometimes rode on the tops of coaches. It had "frightened and distressed him to see them getting down". This getting up and down had to be done in the street, for no coach could then have passed through the archway into the inn yard had it carried outside passengers. Later on, when seats were made for outside travellers, the newer inns built arches sufficiently high to accommodate them. The reason, of course for travelling in this extreme discomfort, was that it was cheap. The outside only paid half the price of an inside seat and he could, if he preferred it, travel in the basket for the same sum. If, driven by rain, snow or extreme discomfort, he wished to change and go inside, he could only do so if one of the insides agreed, and he was then put next to his benefactor.

"ALL GAMMON!"

In 1783 Richard Gammon introduced a bill into the House of Commons to regulate the number of outside passengers—only six might be carried on the roof and two on the box of a three- or four-horsed coach, and on a pair-horse stage only three on the roof and one on the box. " All Gammon ! " infuriated coachmen and coach proprietors exclaimed. Did they not already pay a tax of £5 a year and a halfpenny a mile? The act was a dead letter.

In 1734 one of these new conveyances advertised itself as " The Newcastle Flying Coach ". This marvel actually did the whole journey to London " in nine days, three days sooner than any other coach that travels the road, for which purpose eight stout horses are stationed at proper distances ". Hitherto the coach had gone perhaps twenty-five miles or as far as the unicorn could be induced to draw it, and then had stopped to rest. The passengers stayed at their inn and continued the journey the following day when the horses were thought to be sufficiently refreshed. Now, by changing horses, the journey could be done more expeditiously. Coaches too began to improve, glass replaced boards and leather curtains in the windows and the vehicle was called a glass-coach. Later still the coaches were fitted with springs. This was not always an unmixed blessing. The mail-coaches, of which we shall speak presently, were hung so high that their motion was often intolerable. The landlady of the New London Inn, Exeter, declared that the passengers arriving there in the mails were generally so ill that they went at once to bed without ordering any supper, which was not to the advantage of her house. " Unless " she said " they go back to the old-fashioned coach hung a little lower the mail-coaches will lose all their custom."

These old coaches had no springs, and what the jolting

over those bad roads must have been we cannot conceive. People complained about them, delicate women would not travel in them, the poet Cowper, a timid man, begs for his friends' prayers as he is about to take a journey. Then a few people began to consider improvements. "Friction annihilated" was painted on the axle-box of the "Improved Birmingham Coach" in 1758, which had it been true might have proved even more reassuring than the " *sat cite si sat bene* " which was painted on the door of the Newcastle–London Fly. Then the stage-coach which went from Dean Street, Soho, to Edinburgh in ten days in summer and twelve in winter, advertised that it would "for the better accommodation of passengers be altered to a new genteel two-end glass-coach machine being on steel springs and exceedingly light". Pace was accelerated. Moritz declared it was more like flying than driving and a Dutch traveller from Great Yarmouth to London was so terrified by the speed that he put his head out of the coach window, yelling continuously in his own language, " I must get out, I must get out." " The postillions drive with such speed that it gives me a singing in the ears " another traveller remarked.

John Palmer of Bath had, according to de Quincey, " accomplished two things very hard to do in our little planet. He had invented mail-coaches, and he had married the daughter of a duke."

The first of these mail-coaches set out in 1784, and the Palmer family did very well out of them, amassing what was then the enormous fortune of £100,000. Before this date the mails had been conveyed by post-boys on horseback. This system was most unsatisfactory. Over-ridden horses fell lame or ill, the temptation to linger with a mug of beer over the ale-house fire was too great to be resisted, on lonely country roads the boys were sometimes set upon and robbed. So many letters never reached their destination that correspondents hesitated to use the post. They bribed the driver of a stage-coach to convey letters, though this was against the law, or they entrusted them to travelling friends. Palmer realized that the two requisites for the carriage of letters were speed and safety. The following is the advertisement which he issued in 1784:

MAIL DILLIGENCE

To commence Monday August 2nd. The Proprietors of the above carriage having agreed to convey the mail to and from London and Bristol in sixteen hours with a Guard for its protection respectfully inform the Public that it is constructed so as to accommodate Four Inside Passengers in the most convenient manner, that it will set off every Night at Eight o'clock from the Swan with Two Necks Lad's Lane London, and arrive at the Three Tuns Inn Bath before Ten the next Morning and at the Runner Tavern Bristol at Twelve. Will set off at the said Tavern at Bristol at four o'clock every Afternoon, and arrive at London at Eight o'clock. The Price to and from Bristol, Bath and London twenty eight shillings for each Passenger. No Outsides allowed. Both the Guard and the Coachman, who will be likewise armed, have given ample security to the Proprietors for their conduct, so that those Ladies and Gentlemen, who may be pleased to honour them with their Encouragement, may depend upon every Respect and Attention.

Whatever respect and attention they may have paid the passengers, the armed guard of the mail-coach could be a terror on the roads. Pennant writing in 1792 declares that " these guards shoot at dogs, hogs, sheep and poultry as they pass the road, and even in towns to the great terror and danger of the inhabitants ". On one occasion a guard went so far as to shoot a toll-keeper.

The old stage-coaches had no guards. The coachman, indeed, possessed a blunderbuss concealed somewhere in the box, but he did not often use it. The post-office appointed and paid the guards of the mails and provided them with cutlasses and a blunderbuss which had a folding bayonet attached. The sight of such things was apt to go to a man's head, and if there were no highwaymen to shoot he aimed at a cock or a hog, occasionally he hit. These men had low wages, they depended on tips or more questionable sources for income. Parcels and letters were put into their hands and not into the post and they would deliver them for less than the post-office charged. This was generally winked at by the mail-coach superintendents. One of these declared that he had no objection to a guard conveying a joint of meat, and " such a thing as a turtle tied to the roof directed to any gentleman once or twice a year might pass unnoticed, but for a constancy cannot be suffered ". He did protest, however, when a guard used a mail-bag for carrying fish or put 150 lb. of meat and ice into the coach-box. It was, he considered, a little too much, people were complaining of an ancient and fish-like smell. By these means guards did fairly well and on good routes might make £400 or £500 a year. Some coachmen made as much or more, others, drivers of stage-coaches on out-of-the-way routes, fared very badly. The night coaches were the worst of all. In early days, as we have said, there had been no night travelling. Coach passengers were dragged out of their beds at five in the morning and deposited, shaky and tottering, at an inn at nine o'clock in the evening. Then night coaches were put on the roads. Anything was considered good enough for them, horses with the staggers, harness in decay, cushions with the moth in them, wheels which came off. No one travelled by a night coach if he could help it and the unfortunate driver sometimes made no more than 12s. a week. Two shillings or half a crown was the usual tip to a coachman. " How much do you expect ? " said an innocent passenger to a coachman. " Gents generally gives me a shilling, fools with more money than brains two and six " was the honest, if caustic, reply. Few would have dared give as little as a shilling, though Dr. Johnson scolded Boswell for giving as much. Coachmen were not to be trifled with, as they sat up aloft on the box seat, clad in many caped coats and fancy waistcoats, sipping brandy and water brought from the inn by obsequious attendants. In the eyes of sporting youth there was something glamourous about them, even if they reeked of spirits and had filed off their front teeth to be the better able to deal with the whip-cords, which they always carried in their mouths. Many a young man paid extra for a seat beside the coachman and would gladly give a guinea to be allowed to drive a good four-in-hand along a smooth road. A coachman was liable to a fine of from five to ten pounds for allowing passengers to drive and the common informer, who was so rife in the eighteenth century, was often lurking behind a hedge. These common informers were common pests. They were of course remunerated by the fines extracted from their victims, and some of them actually formed themselves into societies or, one might say, unlimited companies with their spies on every road and attorneys in their pay. Still the coachman, with that reckless disregard of the law and its consequences so characteristic of the age, would often pass the ribbons into other hands, smoke a pipe or take snuff and talk horses, while the young man who had slipped speedily on to the box seat had realized his ambition. We do not know whether he paid the coachman's heavy fine if the matter ever came into court. The men who drove the mail-coaches were a brave, hardy race, many of them great characters. It is pleasant to think that Mr. Weller, senior, must have driven a coach over the roads of the eighteenth century. Another driver, William Salter, drove the Yarmouth stage-coach and has his epitaph in the churchyard of Haddiscoe, near Lowestoft:

> Here lies Will Salter, honest man
> Deny it Envy if you can
> True to his Business and his Trust
> Always punctual, always just
> His horses, could they speak, would tell
> They loved their good old master well
> His uphill work is chiefly done
> His Stage is ended, Race is won
> One Journey is remaining still
> To climb up Sion's holy Hill
> And now his faults are all forgiven
> Elija like drive up to Heaven
> Take the Reward of all his Pains
> And leave to other hands the Reins.

On a fine summer's day on good roads and when seats had been provided, a drive on the top of a coach could be extremely pleasant. Even the names of the vehicles were exciting. There were Telegraphs, Highfliers, Balloon coaches, Defiances and more sober-sounding Hopes, Perseverances, Regulators and Good Intents. On May Day they would be decked with flowers, with holly at Christmas and for a victory with laurel. As the coach drove into a town or village the guard would play a tune on his horn. The inhabitants could set their clocks and watches by the mail-coaches for they kept excellent time. Coachmen were fined if they were late and at the end of the century often carried a chronometer in a leather case. The stage-coach drivers never bothered about punctuality.

In 1737 there was a coach which advertised that it went from London to Exeter in three days; but everyone knew that it took about six. The mail-coaches, towards the end of the century, might do as much as seven miles an hour on tolerable roads; but the stages did three or four and on bad roads and in bad weather even less. Then the stage-coaches had to stop, or at least slow down at every toll-gate, while the mails, their guard playing Arthur O'Bradley or Blackeyed Susan on his horn, dashed through the gates without paying a groat. Elizabeth Carter, who was fond of taking country walks, had on one occasion resolved to meet a coach at an inn and take it part of the way home. When she reached the inn she found it had already passed; but by walking quickly she was able to catch it up. A stage coachman would generally make room for a chance passenger and put the fare into his own pocket. In the ordinary way it was necessary to secure a seat beforehand, have the name entered in a book and pay down a proportion of the fare. The place where this was done was called a booking-office and the name has persisted into the railway era and down to our own time.

Nearly every foreigner expressed surprise and delight at the comfort of English travel. It must have compared favourably with his own. Englishmen were less enthusiastic. They complained bitterly of being jolted to death, overcharged, cramped and pressed, insulted by the coachman and of the excessive cold in winter. Coach proprietors did what they could. "There was enough straw round my feet to conceal a covey of partridges" one ungrateful passenger remarked. In the early days many coaches laid up for the winter, emerging again on the first of May. When the coach climbed a hill, the male travellers got out and walked. Sometimes they condescended to exchange a few words with the outsides, letting it be known that they would not speak to such low fellows when they came to their inn. The behaviour of the travelling Englishman is well described by Count Kielmansegg.

" The first sight of people of different classes and sexes, who are perfectly unknown to each other, occasions, at the outset, deep silence, as nobody knows what to make of his neighbour or how to begin a conversation. At last someone begins to talk of the road and the weather; this gradually brings up other subjects, such as how long one is on the road etc. A political discussion is sure to follow especially with English people."

The Count, when he wrote thus, had just been subjected to a vexatious delay at Godalming, as the Duke of York and Prince Charles of Mecklenburg had taken all the horses from the inn. He had had to travel in a " flying-machine " which he evidently considered beneath his dignity, though he was consoled by finding a Captain Campbell of the East India service, who was related to the Duke of Argyll, reduced to the same extremity.

This flying-machine probably resembled the one described as follows:

" The Colchester Machine seating 6 persons inside, in front outside behind the coachman four more, and at the back, where the trunks usually go, as many again within a neat enclosure with benches, while eight people were sitting above on deck, their feet dangling overboard, holding fast by their hands to screwed in brass rings."

The machine certainly never flew. It was indeed a glorified specimen of the stage-waggon. This vehicle was an immense cart with benches inside covered by a canvas or leather hood. It was drawn at foot's pace by eight strong horses and the waggoner walked at their

EIGHTEENTH CENTURY TRANSPORT BY ROAD

heads. It never did more than two miles an hour and only travelled in the day time. Generally the same team of horses pulled the waggon through all its journeys; but the flying waggons changed horses. There was the Shrewsbury Flying Waggon which began flying from Shrewsbury to London in 1750. This took five days to travel 152 miles. These heavy waggons cut up the roads, and after 1766 they were compelled to have wheels not less than sixteen inches broad and a bonus was given to those which were over two feet in breadth. A few years later James Sharpe of London made waggon wheels so broad that they rolled the roads, and the vehicle was known as the rolling waggon. People travelled in these slow-moving, uncomfortable carts because they were cheap. The charge was 1*d*. or 1½*d*. a mile, whereas the stage-coaches charged 3*d*. or 4*d*. a mile.

Travellers, who went in their own carriages, could take as much luggage as the vehicle would hold and the horses could draw. Sometimes, distrustful of inn furnishings, they conveyed their own mattresses and bed linen and even canteens of plate. The coaches had to limit the amount of luggage which passengers might take with them. Fourteen pounds weight was usually carried free; anything over this amount was charged a penny a pound and heavy luggage was refused. The cost of carriage by the waggon was very high; 40*s*. a ton would have been charged for the carriage of goods between Manchester and Liverpool, though they could be sent by water for 12*s*.

" A traveller on foot in this country " says Pastor Moritz " seems to be considered a sort of wild man or an out-of-the-way being, who is stared at, pitied, suspected and shunned by everybody that meets him."

Moritz did not suffer from this treatment merely because he was a foreigner. Richard Warner, an English clergyman, who was so eccentric as to go on walking tours, met with gross rudeness from inn-keepers and jeers and missiles from small boys. It was supposed that no man of substance would ever walk, except with a gun over his shoulder, and that everyone who tramped the roads was either a footpad or a pauper. The roads were generally in such a bad state that walking could not have been pleasant and there was always the danger of attacks from footpads. It was not till the early nineteenth century when the highways were improved and robbers were less numerous, that walking became the pleasure and pastime of all classes.

Coaches were forbidden to travel on a Sunday, though the law was sometimes disregarded. So little travelling was there, however, that highwaymen did not consider it worth while to go out on Sundays. Grosley, marooned at Dover with a number of other passengers, found coachmen willing to drive them to London.

" The great multitude of passengers " he says " with which Dover was then crowded, afforded a reason for dispensing with a law of the police by which public carriages are in England forbid to travel on Sunday. I myself set out on a Sunday with seven more passengers in two carriages called 'flying machines'. These vehicles, which are drawn by six horses, go twenty-eight leagues a day from Dover to London for a guinea. Servants are entitled to a place for half the money, either behind the coach or on the coach-box, which has three places. The coachmen, whom we changed every time with our horses, were lusty, well made, dressed in good cloth. When they set off or were for animating the horses, I heard a sort of periodical noise, resembling that of a stick striking against the nave of the forewheel, customary with English coachmen to give their horses the signal for setting off."

By 1777 Messrs. Pickford had already started a career which has lasted to the present time, as the following advertisement in *Prescott's Manchester Journal* will show:

"This is to acquaint all Gentlemen and others that M. Pickford's Flying Waggons go to London in Four Days and a Half. M. Pickford will not be accountable for any Money, Plate, Watches, Jewels, Writing, Glass, China, etc. unless entered as such and paid for accordingly."

It was not only the poor who travelled by these stage-waggons or caravans as they were sometimes called. Middle-class persons, especially women travelling alone, often preferred them. The highwaymen scorned them as beneath their notice. It is true the waggons carried goods and luggage, but these were usually heavy, bulky articles, too big and weighty for the coaches. It is probable, as Messrs. Pickford's advertisement suggests, that some people entrusted plate, watches and jewellery to their care. Highwaymen on horseback could not remove anything big or heavy, nor could they spend time examining luggage, it would have been too risky. Their policy was to snatch watches, jewellery or purses from the unlucky travellers, and then ride hastily away. The foreign visitor would not use the waggon except in cases of necessity like Count Kielmansegg or when, like Pastor Moritz, he had to consider ways and means. If he did not travel by it he probably dispatched his heavy luggage in it or, from a port, there were often facilities for sending it by sea, from inland towns by river and by the canals which intersected England. Much merchandise was carried by water, since the rivers had been deepened and supplied with locks, and Brindley had begun to make canals. This water traffic, as Dr. Trevelyan points out, led to a great increase in foreign trade, and consequently, we may infer, in the number of foreign travellers in England.

Travelling by water had its dangers and discomfort. " Gott sei dank ! " von Uffenbach ejaculated when he came safely up the river from Greenwich. He tells us that when he got to London Bridge he " got out and walked, leaving the boatmen to row through alone, for the stream is so strong that boats are often upset there ".

De Saussure writes that there were 15,000 boats to be hired on the Thames in London. The inhabitants liked this method of transport. There might be some danger at London Bridge, and there were sometimes collisions on the congested waterway ; but on a fine day it was easy and tranquil, the passengers by boat glided pleasantly along, avoiding the cobbled streets, the ruts and pitfalls of suburban roads, the attentions of highwaymen.

CHAPTER 3

Roads, Tolls and Highwaymen

IN the year 1702 King Charles III of Spain decided to adventure himself into that little known and barbarous island called Great Britain. Accordingly he sailed with his suite to Portsmouth, and from there the company was conveyed as far as Petworth in Sussex, where they waited for the Queen's husband, Prince George of Denmark, who was to meet them and escort them to Windsor. His experiences on this journey of forty miles, which occupied fourteen hours, are thus described by one of the attendants.

"We set out at six in the morning by torchlight to go to Petworth and did not get out of our coaches (save only when we were overturned or stuck fast in the mire) till we arrived at our journey's end. 'Twas hard service for the Prince to sit fourteen hours in a coach that day without eating anything and passing through the worst ways I ever saw in my life. We were thrown but once indeed in going, but our coach, which was the leading one, and his Highness's body coach would have suffered very much if the nimble boors of Sussex had not frequently poised it or supported it with their shoulders from Godalming almost to Petworth; and the nearer we approached the Duke of Somerset's house the more inaccessible it seemed to be. The last nine miles of the way cost us six hours to conquer them; and indeed we had never done it if our good master had not, several times, lent us a pair of horses out of his own coaching whereby we were able to trace out the road for him."

It seems indeed extraordinary that Prince George was obliged to go without food for fourteen hours. If there was no inn on the road of sufficient consequence to entertain a Prince, any nobleman or country squire, whose seat they passed, would have welcomed him. Hospitality was often thus extended to total strangers who might be stranded upon the road; but perhaps the Prince did not wish to keep the King of Spain waiting at Petworth.

"I looked like a crazy creature when I entered the metropolis" Pastor Moritz writes after one of his journeys. He had come up in the day from Northampton, and "could hardly call it a journey but rather perpetual motion or removal in a closed box".

Upon no subject were travelling Englishmen more unanimously eloquent than upon the shocking condition of the roads.

"I know not, in the whole range of language, terms sufficiently expressive to describe this infernal road" says that great traveller Arthur Young, about a road which he had just traversed in Lancashire.

"The roads grew bad, beyond all badness, the night dark, beyond all darkness, the guide frightened beyond all frightfulness" says Horace Walpole speaking of a journey from Tonbridge to Penshurst. The roads, in many parts of England, were very bad. In Sussex they were generally so impassable in winter that the judges on circuit refused to hold the assizes at Lewes, the county town. They struggled down as far as Guildford or Horsham and waited there for prisoners, constables and jurymen to plough through the mud as best they might. In Devon there were no roads west of Exeter, which could be used for wheeled traffic. " This infernal road was most execrably vile with ruts four feet deep" is Arthur Young's description of a road between Preston and Wigan. There is no doubt that the state of the highways varied very much and that as the century progressed they were, in some cases, greatly improved. Early in the eighteenth century it was still the custom to repair the roads by statute labour and all parishioners were called on to contribute to their upkeep. The squire and the farmer were obliged to send a certain number of horses and carts; labourers had to contribute six days work in the year. The way-warden, who was an unpaid official chosen by the local magistrates, was supposed to superintend their labour. At times, when he had nothing better to do or when the local squire made a fuss about it, he may have infused a little energy into the workmen. More often he would join them in consuming the beer which thoughtful parish vestries generally provided. In the spring, when the road-ploughs went out and scraped away the winter's accumulation of mud and stones, very little improvement could be discerned. Farmers were always grumbling at having to lend waggons and horses. It was never convenient to part with them, and six days' work on the roads caused more damage than six months' work upon the farm. Labourers protested, in spite of much beer, that they were hardly used. In many parishes it became the custom to accept payment in money. Instead of lending his waggon, a squire or farmer might pay the sum of £1 10s. towards the upkeep of the roads, and in time a sort of highway rate was evolved. A man who paid a rent of £50 was considered as a possessor of a waggon and four horses and was charged accordingly. The roads, for the most part, remained as bad as ever. Telford and Macadam, those great engineers, were the first men to understand how a road should be made.

Before their time it was usual to throw a few large stones into the ruts and potholes and even that was not always done. People were resigned to the state of the highways. They had never known anything better. One country squire, despairing of any improvement, measured the width between his native ruts and had his carriage designed accordingly. If a neighbourhood had very bad roads, travellers avoided it. In some parts even a cart was a rarity.

"Dorchester" we read in the *Gentleman's Magazine* of 1739 "is to us a terra incognito and the map makers might, if they pleased, fill the vacuities of Devon and Cornwall with forests, sands, elephants, savages and what they please."

It is a curious commentary on continental highways that most foreigners should have praised our roads. Even Grosley, who disliked many things in England, says nothing about that road from Dover to London, over which he went and of which Arthur Young, writing about the same time, declares that "it would be a prostitution of language to call a turnpike". "These roads are magnificent, being wide, smooth and well kept" says Cesar de Saussure, the Swiss traveller from Lausanne, who came to England in 1784. "The road (from Harwich to London) is always kept in good order with fine gravel and sand, and the slightest unevenness is mended at once" is a description by Count Kielmansegg. "Incomparable" was Moritz's comment on the roads of England, and Alfieri was "astonished and, delighted with the excellence of the highways and the beauty of the horses". Casanova also speaks of the goodness of the roads and the speed and reasonable cost of travel.

As the century advanced the authorities began to consider the question of turnpikes. In days before universal rating or highway boards the idea was not a bad one. Everyone who travelled, except foot passengers, paid for the roads. If the government had kept the turnpikes in its own hands, there would, doubtless, have been peculation and inefficiency; but it might have been better than the system which was adopted. This was to farm out the turnpikes to various bodies known as trusts who bought the roads by auction and made what they could out of them. These turnpike trusts were set up all over the country. There were high white gates at every five miles or so of the principal roads with the curiously shaped, minute houses, of which many survive to the present day. From these the turnpike men ran out whenever they heard the sound of horses hooves or of wheels upon the road. At night the wretched men might be roused several times by knocks upon the door and window, and cries of " Pike, Gate, Hallo ". No wonder they became bad-tempered and morose, inclined to charge more than they should and browbeat the poor. Every vehicle except the mail-coaches paid toll and even animals driven along the road. A rider on horseback paid $1\frac{1}{2}d$. at each toll-gate, a cart or carriage with one horse paid $4\frac{1}{2}d$. and a four-in-hand 1s. 6d. Cattle, sheep and pigs were paid for by the score. A list of tolls was displayed at each toll-house; but as many could not read, the keeper often charged what he pleased. The turnpike trusts were very unpopular. To stop every five miles or so and pay out good money was extremely irksome, and the roads did not seem to be much improved. Infuriated mobs set upon the toll-gates and houses and in some cases pulled them down. In Yorkshire the soldiers were called out to quell a serious popular outbreak against the obnoxious trusts. The drivers of waggons and flocks and herds avoided the toll-gates when they could. The beasts were driven through the fields, the waggons went on the side roads, which were still kept up by the parish. After protests from the turnpike trusts, this latter practice was made illegal. Any waggoner thus avoiding the turnpikes was liable to forfeit " one horse not being the shaft or thill horse, and all his gear and accoutrements ", but the penalty was not often enforced. The beasts were generally driven through the fields. It had been the custom from earliest times and though farmers might grumble and talk about trespass, English custom was too strong for them, and foot passengers had always the right to walk on adjacent land if the highway was impassable.

About the middle of the eighteenth century milestones replaced, on many roads, the old crosses which had been put up in ancient times to mark the tracks. There were other stones which showed the boundaries of a turnpike trust and on hills there were stones marked " put on ". This signified that another horse was allowed for the hill without any extra charge being made by the turnpike authorities. On the top of the hill would be another stone marked " take off ". The milestones appealed to the German traveller. English miles were shorter than the German, and he had the illusion that he was journeying much faster than he expected. Some travellers complained that the mile-stones were inaccurate. Probably they varied in different parts of the country. " This place (Leicester)[1] is called seventy-eight miles from London " says Sarah Duchess of Marlborough writing to her daughter, " but the miles are so long in this country that I am sure that it is a great deal more ".

On the road from Salisbury to Shaftesbury there were no mile-stones; but Lord Pembroke had had a tree

---

[1] Leicester is $97\frac{3}{4}$ miles from London.

planted at every mile of the way. This would not be of much use nowadays; but in the eighteenth century in unenclosed country there was no hedgerow timber. Signposts were very few, and in many parts of the country non-existent. It was often absolutely necessary to hire a guide for the journey, if travelling otherwise than by stage or mail. John Metcalf, Blind Jack of Knaresborough as he was called, who had walked from London to York and marched in the '45 from York to Scotland, was one of the best guides over the moors. Others, though possessed of sight, were by no means so reliable and guided their parties into swamps or to wrong destinations.

The treatment of horses seems to have varied as did the beasts themselves. The fast mail-coaches had very good teams and the coachmen were proud of their animals. They were often renewed and if the work proved too much for them they were sold to tradesmen and others where they would have an easier time. "The coach whip" says Grosley "is no more in their hands than a fan is, in winter, in the hands of a lady . . . their horses scarce ever feel it."

"Certainly in no part of Europe are horses better fed, better housed or more attended to" Meister declares, though this was after visiting the stables of a large country house. "A hell for horses and a heaven for women" was another and as regard the horses perhaps a truer commentary. On the old slow coaches and the night coaches conditions were very bad. Any aged, spavined, broken-down beast would be put to this sort of work and the drivers had to get them along the roads somehow. Many, it is to be feared, used a horrible thing called a "short Tommy", a sort of cat-o'-nine-tails. There was no Society for the Prevention of Cruelty to Animals, no laws for their protection. John

Woolman the American Quaker, who was one of the first to protest against slavery, protested also vehemently against cruelty to horses. He insisted upon walking the whole distance from London to Yorkshire, though it took him six weeks to do so, and he died from the effect of the journey. He would not countenance the cruelty which he saw by travelling in a coach. " Stage coaches " he says " frequently go upwards of one hundred miles in twenty-four hours and I have heard Friends say in several places that it is common for horses to be killed with hard driving and that many others are driven till they go blind . . . so great is the hurry in the spirit of this world that in aiming to do business quickly and to gain wealth the creation at this day doth loudly groan."

Grosley, on the other hand, comments on the humanity of the English and the kindness of both riders and blacksmiths towards the horses, though he admits that that good treatment did not extend to asses.

Cesar de Saussure tells us how he hired a horse which he calls a sorry jade. It took him, however, from London to Guildford and back in one day, without using whip or spur. He rode it, he says, at a hard gallop, except upon the stones and pavement.

" England " de la Rochefoucauld declares " is perhaps the only country where you may travel with your own horses, without a man to look after them. You may rely on their getting the best treatment in the world. Inn-keepers indeed will bestow such attention upon them as can be accounted for only by the national affection for the horse."

Englishmen might not have agreed with him. When putting up at an inn an Englishman always sent his servant to see that the horses were properly fed and cared for. If he were travelling alone he went himself to see that his mount was comfortable. The care and nurture of the horse was indeed part of the education of an English gentleman. English horses were highly prized on the Continent. Alfieri, the Italian dramatist, came here to buy horses. He purchased fourteen for which he paid large sums. Ill luck, however, attended his purchase; one horse coughed, another fell lame, a third refused to eat and the amount he spent getting them home to Italy across Mont Cenis, and their sustenance and upkeep during five years, exhausted the large sums of money which he had in the French funds.

Besides the roads there were tracks over the country where the pack-horses went. Itinerant merchants loaded their horses at Stourbridge or some other large fair, and set off over pack-horse roads and bridges to sell their wares in country towns and villages. As many as thirty or forty of these small, sturdy creatures would proceed in a string, the leader wearing a bell to warn other pack-horse owners of their approach through the narrow ways with their high banks. In some parts of the country these tracks were the only way of getting about the country and everything was carried by the horses in panniers or sometimes drawn in a narrow sledge.

In the early days of the century there was little Sunday travelling. Coaches did not run except occasionally from Dover to London if the amount of passengers was very great. It was indeed sometimes possible to hire post-horses. Grosley did so, but such a thing was evidently unusual even upon the Dover Road. "We were a sort of show" he says " to the inhabitants of the several towns and villages through which we posted." Sunday travelling was expensive, the hire of horses was doubled and the toll-gates on the outskirts of London charged two or even three times their usual charges. Towards the end of the century Sunday travelling increased. Brighton, now becoming a fashionable resort, was the first place from which a coach ran to London on a Sunday. Expensive though it might be to travel on this day, people would occasionally do it. Highwaymen were taking their weekly rest, and the roads were safe from their attentions. They did not consider it worth their while to ride out on a Sunday.

Perhaps the palmy days of the highwaymen were in the seventeenth century, when the roads were even worse than in the eighteenth, the coaches slower, and no attempt had been made to police the highways. There were only four really famous highwaymen in the eighteenth century—Dick Turpin, Claude Duval, Captain McLean and Jack Rann. Dick Turpin's history does not bear looking into; he is a sorry disappointment. He was a deer stealer, a horse thief and a burglar, and if he ever robbed the traveller it must have been only occasionally and in his spare time. He never rode from London to York; that famous feat was performed by an enterprising gentleman in the previous century. Captain McLean, who robbed Horace Walpole, was more romantic. He was the son of a clergyman and had very good manners. Respectable people, ignorant of his profession, invited him into their houses, where he stole the hearts of their daughters. We are not told if he stole anything else, but it is not probable, the highwayman had usually a profound contempt for the sneak thief, and pickpocket, nor did he really think much of burglars. The most picturesque of the four was Jack Rann or Sixteen-string Jack as he was called, because his breeches had eight strings of various colours at each knee. He had begun life as a postillion and then became a coachman, so he knew the roads well. When he came before Sir John Fielding on a charge of highway robbery, he wore an enormous bunch of flowers in his coat and had his irons decorated with blue ribbons. Asked by the magistrate if he had anything to say, he replied with a ready insolence, " I know no more of the matter than you do or half as much." He was acquitted on that occasion for lack of evidence and repaired a day or two later to Bagnigge Wells, a place of entertainment and evil reputation near London. He wore a scarlet coat, white silk stockings and a laced hat, and proclaimed himself as Sixteen-string Jack the Highwayman. When he was arrested for robbing Princess Amelia's chaplain he appeared in court in a pea-green coat, ruffled shirt and a hat with silver strings, and while waiting execution he had several girls to dine with him in Newgate. He kept up the picturesque highwayman tradition which was immortalized in *The Beggar's Opera*; but the German traveller Lichtenberg seems to think that it was not what it had been. " The English highwaymen " he says sadly " have lost their magnanimity." What caused this melancholy reflection, whether the attack by a highwayman on Lord North or the fact that he used firearms, is not clear.

Another traveller seems to have heard of the tradition, but knew nothing of it from personal experience. " I have been told " he said " that some highwaymen are quite polite and generous, begging to be excused for being forced to rob, and leaving passengers the wherewithall to continue their journey."

These gentlemen of the road, however generous they may have been upon occasion, were undoubtedly a serious menace to the countryside and even to the towns. Von Uffenbach, the German scholar, who was in England in 1710, returned late one night from Richmond to London. He confessed that he was " in considerable terror of being robbed. It is no small scandal " he says " that in so mighty a realm and such a capital, one can feel no security even in the vicinity of a town ... such robberies take place at night in the town itself and even in the neighbourhood of St. James's Palace." Hogarth's engraving *Night*, we may remember, depicts a coach being held up in a crowded street in London, and a highwayman firing through the window. The crowd do not seem to be regarding the attack as anything out of the way or doing anything about it. Count Kielmansegg tells us how he had been invited to dine with one of the City Companies near Gray's Inn.

" We took the road round the town " he says " which was more convenient than going through the City ; but we provided ourselves with an armed servant on horseback, because my Lady Huntingdon had been robbed a few days previously of her watch and money by a highwayman in those parts. We remained close together in our three carriages and divided our party so that we drove in pairs."

Highwaymen had often their own particular beats. There was Claude Duval who robbed and danced on Hounslow Heath, Johnnie Abershaw who frequented the Surrey commons, the Golden Farmer who looked after the Exeter road. Many of these men had been soldiers and when peace came they found themselves thrown upon a cold world, having lost any aptitude or taste for work which they might formerly have had. Sometimes a bankrupt tradesman would take to the road. Sophie de la Roche tells us how she, with a party of friends, were held up by a single highwayman. One of them, a young lady, seeing that the robber was young and shy and obviously new to the job, remonstrated with him and pointed out the probable end of his career. Sophie says that he thanked her for her kindness and rode away without robbing them. On the next day the ladies collected 150 guineas between them and put an advertisement in the papers saying that he might have the money if he called for it. The highwayman arrived full of contrition and gratitude, vowing that the young lady's voice " had resounded in him like an angel's and had moved his soul ". He took the money, paid his more pressing debts and went to an uncle in the country who received him, promised to help him and " blessed the lady ". It was another of the pleasant adventures which befell the delightful Sophie. Besides an armed guard, travellers adopted other means of circumventing highwaymen. " We English " said Sir Augustus Hervey to Casanova " always carry two purses on our journeys, a small one for the robbers and a large one for ourselves." Casanova took the advice and when he was travelling to London from Lord Pembroke's he put six guineas for highwaymen in a separate purse. He was, however, not attacked. Other people collected bad money and offered it to robbers; some had boots made with cavities in the heel in which they put their valuables and hid their money about their persons. This, however, was not always of much use, for if the highwaymen found nothing, they would sometimes search the travellers.

There were many complaints about the dangers of the roads, and some efforts were made to mitigate them. The turnpike men in their toll-houses were provided with speaking trumpets that they might give warning of the approach of robbers. A reward of £40 was offered for the arrest of a highwayman attacking a stage-coach, £200 was given to anyone apprehending a robber of the mail and as much as £300 if the attack was made within five miles of London. Few highwaymen tried to rob the mails openly, the guards were well armed, and it was too dangerous. They often abstracted goods or parcels in the inn yard before the coach started, or while they were changing horses, if the guard's attention could be diverted. The high rewards offered no doubt led to the apprehension of many highwaymen, but it also encouraged the informer. Readers of Fielding will remember the classic example of Jonathan Wild; and there were many more of his trade. In 1768 five men made a kind of syndicate, and having persuaded some poor wretches to rob the coaches, they collected as much as £960 in rewards.

Towards the end of the century the roads undoubtedly became safer. Near London the Bow Street Runners, precursors of Peel's police, affected many arrests, and a few other large towns had a similar force. Bank notes, which could be more easily concealed and cheques which were useless to highwaymen, took the place of the bags of gold, which merchants and others had been compelled to carry. Fire-arms were improved, the old blunderbuss, which generally misfired, was replaced with more lethal weapons, and as highwaymen sadly complained, travellers were not slow to use them. The days when the highwaymen were kings of the road, with innkeepers and ostlers in their pay, were nearly over.

Even as early as the middle of the century improvements of all kinds had been made and the English scene had changed. A contributor to the *Gentleman's Magazine* writes in 1754, " Were the same persons, who made a full tour of England thirty years ago, to make a fresh one now, they would find themselves in a land of enchantment. England is no more like to what England was than it resembles Borneo or Madagascar."

The romantic revival which was exemplified in Horace Walpole's *Castle of Otranto* and the publication of the *Percy Reliques*, led to an ever growing interest in ancient buildings and to a desire for travel and exploration. This desire spread even to the Continent and brought travellers to our shores who were drawn there, not by the attraction of business, the lure of learning or the ties of kindred, but by a curiosity to see the island of whose beauties they had heard so much.

CHAPTER 4

Inns, Lodgings, Coffee-Houses and Clubs

THE first necessity for the traveller on arrival was to look for a place in which to stay. Unless he was going directly to friends, he had the choice of stopping at an inn, finding lodgings, or hiring a furnished house. There was no difficulty about finding an inn. In many cases the landlord himself would meet the boats, and persuade the foreign travellers to follow him. At Harwich, we are told, an enterprising landlord seized a passenger's overcoat and hurrying in front of him, led him triumphantly to the Three Cups, where, the passenger, Count Kielmanscgg tells us, " we found everything we could wish for, a good cup of tea, bread and butter and well-aired, clean beds ". If the landlord did not meet the arrivals, it was not difficult for them to find an inn. It was one of the most important buildings in the town, with a wide archway leading to the yard where there were often three tiers of galleries. Inn signs were of enormous size. Grosley comments on this and on " the ridiculous magnificence of the ornaments with which they are overcharged and the height of a sort of triumphal arch which supports them, and most of which cross the street ". The few of these " triumphal arches " which survive are very beautiful, and the signs themselves were often extremely ancient.

The oldest of all was the Bush which the good wine did not need. This was the ivy bush, which, it is said, came with the Romans to Britain and denoted the worship of Bacchus. The traveller would be struck with the hosts of Dragons, Bulls, Bears, Swans, Lions, Sugar Loaves and Peacocks, which abounded, though, to be sure, their counterparts existed on the Continent. "The Ship and Shovel" struck him as peculiar. Was there ever an inn called the Shovel, and had it joined forces with the Ship and why was there a man's head on it? He would have been told, if he had asked, that the Shovel denoted the Sir Cloudesley Shovel, who was, besides a great admiral, the friend and supporter of the common sailor. The Green Man was surprising too; who could know that he was the gamekeeper and that his green clothes were an early form of camouflage. The Bull and Mouth, some have thought, was a corruption of Boulogne Mouth; but it is quite probable that it was the union of two inns, the Bull and the Mouth. In the same way the Goat and Compasses may have been the result of a similar fusion, though we are told that it descended from the Puritan motto "God encompasseth us". The traveller from Catholic countries might have been surprised to find in that very Protestant England, several Maid's Heads, some Virgins, a Pilgrim's Rest, a St. Peter's Finger and many George and Dragons.

The traveller had his choice of inns but must select them with care. There were, first, the grand establishments, the Posting Houses, which entertained the quality who posted in their own carriages or in post-chaises. They might accommodate riding gentlemen if these were duly accompanied by their servants. Some of these inns accepted passengers from the mail-coach, some did not; but they never stooped so far as to take in the common stage. Those low people had to go to the inns which catered for them; but they had the satisfaction of knowing that there were others of a still inferior order. The passenger in the waggon, the walker on foot, was seldom admitted or, if he were, was pushed into the kitchen and fed upon remains. Some protested, like Pastor Moritz, who did not see why his money should not be as good as another's. "As I entered the inn (at Windsor)" he says "and desired to have something to eat, the countenance of the waiter soon gave me to understand that I should there find no very friendly reception. Whatever I got they seemed to give me with such an air, as showed too plainly how little they thought of me, and as if they considered me but as a beggar. I must do them justice to own, however, that they suffered me to pay like a gentleman. No doubt this was the first time that this pert, bepowdered puppy had ever been called upon to wait on a poor devil who entered their place on foot." Moritz was shown a room which he said "resembled a prison for malefactors", and when he asked for a better one he was told that they had no room for such guests, and that he had better go back to Slough. For such accommodation he had to pay nine shillings, which included supper on an old tough fowl, and the share of a room with a drunken man who got into bed in his boots. The good pastor would have done as well at a hedge-inn, and probably have been charged a tenth of the price. His bill was preposterous, the landlord was evidently set upon fleecing a foreigner.

The hedge-inns, who took wayfarers and waggon passengers, charged about 9*d.* or 1*s.* for bed and supper. There was one where Swift slept on his way from Moor Park to Leicester which charged only 6*d.* for a clean bed to himself. At another hostelry Moritz found that, when he had put on clean linen and spruced himself up, he was taken into the parlour instead of the kitchen, and was even addressed as "sir" instead of "master". At the Mitre at Oxford he found "princelike attendance", but then, though he came on foot, he was introduced by an Oxford clergyman.

Even in good inns it was not unusual for total strangers to share rooms or even beds. This was regarded in much the same way as the sharing of a ship's cabin at the present day. The unfortunate Grosley was turned out of his bed at 3 a.m. to make room for another traveller. The inns at the ports catered for foreigners, who might often be detained there for days waiting for a favourable wind. The landlord could sometimes talk a little French and German, and one enterprising host at Dover kept a library of books in several languages to beguile the time of the windbound traveller. There were inns in London which took in only foreigners. There was the German inn in Suffolk Street where Sophie de la Roche stayed, and a French house, La Sabonière in Leicester Fields. There they were all the time in the company of their fellow countrymen, which is the aim of so many travellers, and did not have to talk that detestable English which they found so difficult. They had their own food too, the cooking and the wines of France and Germany, which they were sure were better than anything this country could offer.

On the whole, however, the English inns were good. Arthur Young, who had travelled through the length and breadth of England and had said many nasty things about English inns, became enthusiastic about them when he was on French soil. "Go" he said "in England to towns that contain 1,500, 2,000 or 3,000 people in situations absolutely cut off from all dependence and almost the expectation of what are properly called travellers, yet you will meet with neat inns, well-dressed and clean people keeping them, good furniture and refreshing civility." He goes on to contrast this with the squalor, poverty, rudeness and bad food to be found at the French inns. He admits that the French beds were better than the English. These were good in England only at first-rate houses.

When the traveller entered an inn he was usually welcomed by the landlord in person, a rubicund man who had often swollen to a vast size from much drinking. The proprietor of a good inn was a man of substance; he ranked above the tradesmen of the town, and Defoe tells us of one who was Mayor of Doncaster, " company for the best gentlemen in the kingdom and who kept a pack of hounds ".

The common dining-room or " coffee room ", as it was called, was an innovation, which came in at the end of the century. In earlier days the traveller had the choice of hiring a private sitting-room or having his meals with the landlord and his family in the parlour or kitchen. This is the explanation of the curious error in *She Stoops to Conquer* when travellers arriving by night at a private house mistake it for an inn.

The gentleman travelling in his own carriage or in a post-chaise always had a private sitting-room. The mail-coach passenger generally did the same and invariably if there were ladies in the party. The stage-coach traveller, however, who ordered a private room was considered to be giving himself airs. Frenchmen and Germans were astonished at the good appointments of the best inns. They found the stairs and landings carpeted. The bedrooms were spacious and clean with good mahogany furniture and immense four-post beds, piled so high with feather mattresses that it needed a short pair of steps to mount into them. There were curtains at the windows and curtains round the beds,

Drawn by W. H. Bartlett
Engraved by J. Le Keux

THE NEW INN, GLOUCESTER

wax candles in the sitting-rooms and pictures on the walls. In one inn, a humble one, where Moritz stayed he found " printed papers with sundry apt and good moral maxims and rules fastened against the room door ... on such wretched paper " he says, " some of the most delightful and finest sentiments may be read—such as would do honour to any writer and any country ". All inns did not confine themselves to fine sentiments and moral maxims; Goldsmith tells us how he wept over *The Babes in the Wood* which he found pasted up on the wall of some inn.

In the principal houses the food was very good. The tables were covered with immense joints; there were fowls, fish, pies and even game, though it was illegal to sell it, and how the landlord got it no one knew or troubled to inquire. Even in the hall there might be glass cases containing hams and saddles of mutton and rounds of beef. In spite of this abundance and comfort the foreign traveller often complained. He thought that the custom of bringing each visitor a pair of slippers on his arrival was a filthy one. He asked why there were no napkins and disliked the idea of wiping his fingers on the tablecloth as the English did. Some travellers thought they had more than enough of cold meat and salad; but after all the great joints had to be finished and English cooks had not the skill of the French in concocting made dishes, nor were they ever popular in England. Macky, the French traveller, complained that when he came to England there was no " ordinary ", and that " you must bespeak a whole dish and pay for the whole, though you eat never so little of it, so that one that cannot feed on one joint must therefore travel dear if he travel single ". Towards the end of the century, when public dining-rooms were introduced into the larger inns, a set dinner became the rule.

Grosley declared that at one inn he could not get anything to eat without going into the kitchen and selecting a steak from the coal fire over which they were broiling. "The sole business of the cook" he says "was to be constantly blowing the sea-coal, which was half extinguished by the fat of the steaks, and to put new steaks in the place of those which the people of the inn came, in succession, to snatch from off the gridiron." Englishmen liked to choose their own steaks and take one which was well cooked or half raw according to his taste. Coffee, the foreigner complained, was like " a prodigious quantity of brown water. Nowhere do people drink worse coffee." Vegetables impregnated with soot were boiled in pans full of water, and lost all their taste and often their colour unless a little copper was put in to keep them green. "The Englishman" Lichtenberg says "after drinking some tepid liquid, cooks his soup in his stomach so that he may be sure that its strength does not evaporate." Soup, however, was not often served. It was considered extravagant, as English cooks knew nothing of the art of making it out of bones and vegetables and the servants, unlike their brethren on the Continent, refused to eat the meat from which it had been made. It is curious that the three things with which the foreigner most often found fault, cooked vegetables, soup and coffee, are those which are most frequently criticized today. We do not seem to have learnt much in culinary art in the last two hundred years. Our meat usually met with praise. "I know nothing more nourishing" says Meister "or that I could eat more frequently without being cloyed, than a good beef steak with potatoes, plumb pudding and good Cheshire cheese." Faujas de St. Fond tells us that he was given "Slices of beef and veal cut very thin and beaten tender, about the size of a hand, sprinkled with bread crumbs, grilled and nicely served on a silver dish, fine big potatoes with salt butter to follow, delicious beer and good Bordeau wine." On the other hand there were travellers who said that the sight of English red " rosbif " made them turn pale. " The Englishman is entirely carnivorous " says Zetzner, " he eats very little bread and calls himself very economical because he spares himself of soup and dessert, which circumstance made me remark that an English dinner is like eternity, it has no beginning and no end."

English dishes were highly seasoned with pepper and other condiments. It was customary to serve honey sauce with beef, and puddings were loaded with sugar. This was not always to the foreigner's taste; but in England, at the beginning of the century, there was no fresh meat in the winter, and what had been salted often needed sauce or condiments to disguise its flavour.

Defoe declared that " the English consume more flesh than half Europe besides " and foreigners seem to have been mostly of this opinion. There were various local dishes. Bath Olivers and Banbury cakes, Devonshire cream, Cornish saffron cake and Melton Mowbray pies are still with us; but there were other varieties which have either entirely disappeared or are little known. In Cambridge the traveller might be regaled with her famous brawn, in Norfolk with cygnet, and at Newbury with crayfish. Laver was served in Somerset, Northumberland had a dish called singing hinnies, and Kent was famous for its huffkins, Cumberland for its hasty pudding and the Sussex downs for wheatears, which Macky declared were like ortolans. You could, moreover, get wonderful cheese at the Bell at Stilton at half a crown a pound. The abundance of food, particularly meat, is noted by many travellers; but Grosley complains that he never got enough to eat in England. " What would be scarce enough for a Frenchman of ordinary appetite " he says " would suffice three hungry Englishmen." He had only two or three slices of bread and butter for breakfast and this had to last till dinner at three or four. Dinner was a very large meal and was generally followed by tea at seven or eight. Supper was eaten by the middle classes and the poor who dined at noon; but those who had a later meal did not often take it. It was considered unwholesome. De Saussure, however, insisted upon having it. He complained of the " plumb porridge, a dish " he says " few foreigners find to their taste . . . a great treat for English people, though I assure you not for me ".

Faujas de St. Fond tells us that " the taste for cleanliness has preserved the use of steel forks with two prongs. They are changed at every course. With regard to little bits of meat which they cannot take hold of, recourse is had to the knife which is broad and rounded at the extremity." In France the three pronged fork was in general use and it came into England during the century; but inns kept to old customs and the two pronger was in existence as late as the nineteenth century.

Travellers seldom stopped at an inn for more than a day or two. If they arrived upon a Saturday they would, as a rule, remain till the Monday, and in such cases were generally the guests of the landlord. People wishing to remain for some time in a place usually took a house, or went into lodgings. Lodgings were generally cheaper than inns. Moritz who had been staying at the Freemason's Tavern in London, where he had paid £1 10*s.* 9*d.* for eight days, including breakfast and dinner, moved to lodgings kept by Germans, " where everything " he tells us " is much more reasonable, and you here eat, drink and lodge for half a guinea a week ". When he was at the Mitre in Oxford he had been obliged, he complains, to pay 3*s.* for supper, bed and breakfast and to give 1*s.*

to the waiter, though at Sutton near Birmingham he had only paid 1s. for the same accommodation and given the chambermaid 4d. "She very civilly thanked me" he adds. Benjamin Franklin took a furnished room in Little Britain, for which he paid 3s. 6d. a week. Later on his landlady, who wanted the protection of a man's presence in the house, made "an abatement of two shillings and thus I continued" Franklin says "to lodge with her during the remainder of my abode in London at eighteen pence a week".

Franklin amazed his fellow workmen in the printing trade by his water-drinking habits. They themselves always drank a pint of beer before breakfast, a pint at breakfast with bread and cheese, another between breakfast and dinner, one at dinner, another at six o'clock and one upon finishing their work. They could not understand how the American Aquatic, as they called him, could do heavier work than they could manage on water alone. They paid every Saturday night a reckoning of four or five shillings for beer, "this cursed beverage" as Franklin called it.

The foreigner was considered fair game by some unscrupulous inn-keepers, but occasionally they overreached themselves. The French Ambassador, who with his suite of twelve stayed for one night at the Red Lion at Canterbury in 1762, was charged the monstrous sum of £44 10s. 8d. As all they had had was lodging and a light supper, he paid the bill with a protest. The story of this imposition spread through London and men travelling the Dover road avoided the Red Lion. Within a few months the landlord put up his shutters. If lodgings were cheaper than inns, and this was usually the case, they had fewer amenities, and the cooking was not generally so good. "Dinner to such lodgers as I am" says Moritz "generally consists of a piece of half boiled or half-roasted meat, and a few cabbage leaves boiled in plain water, on which they pour a sauce made of flour and water. The toast" he adds " is incomparably good." This sauce was in general use, whenever a sauce was thought necessary. It was probably this to which Voltaire referred when he said that " the English had a hundred religions and only one sauce ".

Some travellers merely slept and breakfasted in their lodgings and took their other meals in a tavern. Taverns were to be found only in London and the larger towns. They were in fact the restaurants of those days. They were also the common meeting ground of all men, as Crabbe describes them:

> All the comforts of life in a tavern are known
> 'Tis his home who possesses not one of his own
> And to him who has rather too much of that one
> 'Tis the house of a friend, where he's welcome to run
> The instant you enter the door you're my lord
> With whose taste and whose pleasure I'm proud to accord
> And the louder you call and the longer you stay
> The more I am happy to serve and obey.

The tavern might have a table d'hôte or, as it was called in those days, an ordinary. Prices varied from Pontack's the French house, which charged a guinea for dinner and gave its patrons stewed snails, petits poussins and the best French wines, to the " dive " of which Smollett spoke, where he had " seen many a pretty gentleman with a laced waistcoat dine very comfortably for three pence halfpenny " on tripe, cowheel or sausage. For a shilling a man could get a good dinner at many ordinaries. " Ordinaries " Macky writes " are not so common here as abroad, yet the French have set up two or three for the conveniency of foreigners in Suffolk Street where one is commonly well served." Macky came to England early in the century, by the end of it the ordinary had established itself at most London taverns and a country town inn had its farmer's ordinary on a market day.

Many taverns and chop-houses had their own specialities. There was calipash and calipee at the King's Arms, behind St. Clement's church was a house famed for its mutton chops, and several taverns, notably Dolly's and Betty's in Ivy Lane, specialized in beef steaks and ale. If a man were poor there was an establishment in Moorgate which provided " farthing fries of sausage and black pudding ".

" After dinner and the play or other diversion, the best company " Macky tells us " go to Tom's and Will's Coffee-Houses near adjoining, where there is playing of picquet and the best conversation till midnight. Here you will see blue and green ribbons and stars sitting familiarly with private gentlemen and talking with the same freedom as if they had left their quality and degrees of distance at home, and a stranger tastes with pleasure the universal liberty of speech of the English nation." The coffee-houses had become prominent features in London life. They were to be found in all parts of the metropolis and much business was carried on in them. The greatest number were in the neighbourhood of Drury Lane and Covent Garden and near the Royal Exchange. Newspapers were always provided and, in an age when these were dear, men often came to a coffee-house merely to read them. They would also find paper, pens and ink, and if a man had an abode up two pair of stairs in St. Giles's or some other humble locality, he would often give the coffee-house as his sole address. Some of these places had other attractions. Don Solero's had a museum, which a customer was entitled to see if he had paid as much as 8d. for a snack. Garroway's was celebrated for its wine auctions. Here wine was sold by the candle. An inch of candle was lighted when the sale began and the man who was bidding when the candle flickered out got the wine. At other houses music was the attraction. Lichtenberg writes of one which was frequented by servants, journeymen and apprentices. Every member put down 4*d*. for the evening entertainment " for which he had music and a female singer, anything else had to be paid for separately ". At most coffee-houses there was card playing, and at all reputable ones the play was straight and above board. There were others, however, visited mostly by foreigners and strangers to the metropolis; the wary Londoner avoided them. Macky found himself in one of the worst of these. It was known as Little Man's. " I was never so confounded in my life " he writes " as when I entered into this last. I saw two or three tables full at faro, heard the box and dice rattling in a room upstairs and was surrounded by a set of sharp faces, that I was afraid would have devoured me with their eyes. I was glad to drop two shillings or half a crown at faro to get off with a clear skin and was overjoyed that I had so got rid of them." The coffee-houses which had the sign of a woman's hand holding a coffee-pot were invariably brothels. This was, of course, known to Londoners; but respectable foreigners entering such places, in search of refreshment and innocent recreation, were shocked and embarrassed. Most coffee-houses had their habitual customers, often of a particular trade, profession or politics. " I must not forget to tell you " Macky says " that the parties have their different places, where, however, strangers are always well received; but a Whig will no more go to the Cocoa Tree or Orsinda's than a Tory will be seen at the Coffee-House of St. James's. The Scots generally go to the British and a mixture of all sorts to the Smyrna. There are other little coffee-houses much frequented in this neighbourhood, Young

Man's for officers, Old Man's for stock jobbers, paymasters and courtiers." He might have added that Robbins' and Garraway's attracted City men, that the Chapter Coffee-House had its clientele of booksellers, that Old Slaughters in Martin's Lane attracted its crowd of literary men, when these were not thronging the Bedford or the Turk's Head to listen deferentially to the Great Cham.

The London clubs grew out of the coffee-houses. Grosley tells us that they were not often open to foreigners, but if specially recommended "they meet with all that respect and easy reception so much preferable to ceremony and compliments". De la Rochefoucauld had a poor opinion of clubs. "It is to these clubs" he says "that one must, in large measure, attribute the lack of society in London and the ruin of many families. The club is such a convenient means of social intercourse that it attracts everyone. It is composed of two or three hundred members; usually the number is not fixed. The club-house is always large and well furnished, the tables are always supplied with newspapers, with tea for those who want it and dice for the gamblers. Thus is provided everything that people want. Young men go to the club in their riding-boots, there is nothing to worry them and that is precisely what suits everybody." He adds that club subscriptions were from about five to nine guineas a year and that meals were very expensive. He was speaking, of course, of the clubs of the well-to-do; but there were others. Macky enumerates seven clubs, which he had apparently visited, and tells us that almost every parish had one. "My house" he says "is in Long Acre where every Wednesday and Saturday, a mixture of gentlemen, lawyers and tradesmen meet in a great room and are seldom under a hundred. They have a grave, old gentleman in his own grey hairs, who is their president and sits in an armed chair some steps higher than the rest of their company and keeps the whole room in order. A harp plays all the time at the lower end of the room and every now and then one or other of the company rises and entertains the rest with a song, and by the by, some are good masters. There is nothing drunk but ale, and every gentleman has his separate mug, which he chalks on the table where he sits as it is brought in, and everyone retires when he pleases as from a coffee-house. The room is always so diverted with songs and drinking to one another that there is no room for politics or anything which can sour conversation."

CHAPTER 5

London

THERE can have been few if any travellers who did not stay for at least some days in London. What were their impressions of that great city, and what did they do with themselves when they had eaten their breakfasts in their inns or lodgings? Some, of course, were engaged in business; but even these found time to see the sights and to give their friends some idea of their impressions. Perhaps these had begun before they set foot in the street. The weary traveller may have been awakened every hour by the watch, that band of antiquated police, if such they can be called, who were supposed to arrest criminals. They were seldom on the spot when needed, but never failed to perambulate the streets at night with lantern and staff, proclaiming each hour. It cannot have been conducive to slumber to hear a raucous, quavering voice in the street below informing you that it was

>Past one o'clock and almost two
>My masters all good day to you.

" London " de Saussure tells us, did not possess " any watchmen on foot or on horseback as in Paris, to prevent murder or robbery. The only watchman you see is a man in every street carrying a stick and a lantern, who every time the clock strikes calls out the hour and state of the weather. The first time this man goes his rounds, he pushes the doors of the shops and houses with his stick to ascertain whether they are properly fastened, and if they are not he warns the proprietor."

Then there were the London Cries, immortalized by Wheatley. A few of these began very early in the morning. There was the cry of the poor little chimney sweep going his rounds with his master, and the milk woman with her pails slung from a yoke across her shoulders uttered a queer yodelling cry.

The waggons and drays coming into the London markets made a hideous noise on the cobbled streets. The markets opened very early. Billingsgate at four in summer, and before the actual opening all goods had reached the market.

The unfortunate traveller worn out with a long and fatiguing journey would not have had much sleep. However, having come so far and braved such hardships and dangers, he was determined to go out and see something of the famous city of which he had heard so much. Perhaps he hired a guide or was conducted by friends, or he may have ventured out by himself into the crowded, bustling streets. We complain now of the congestion and din of London traffic. Foreigners made the same complaint a hundred and fifty years ago.

"In the middle of the street" Lichtenberg tells us "roll chaises, carriages and drays in an unending stream. Above this din and the hum and clatter of ten thousand of tongues and feet, one hears the chimes from church towers, the bells of the postmen, the organs, fiddles and hurdy-gurdies and tambourines of English mountebanks, and the cries of those who sell hot and cold viands in the open at the street corners. Then you will see a bonfire of shavings flaring up as high as the upper floors of the houses, in a circle of merrily shouting beggar-boys, sailors and rogues. Suddenly a man, whose handkerchief has been stolen, will cry 'Stop thief' and everyone will begin running and pushing and shoving, many of them not with any idea of catching the thief, but of prigging for themselves perhaps a purse or watch. Before you know where you are a pretty, nicely dressed miss will take you by the hand 'Come my lord, come along, let us drink a glass together' or 'I'll go with you, if you please.' Then there is an accident forty paces from you. 'God bless me!' cries one. 'Poor creature!' another. Then one stops and must put one's hand in one's pocket for all appear to sympathize with the misfortunes of the poor creature; but all of a sudden they are laughing again because someone has laid down by mistake in the gutter. 'Look there, damn me' says a third and the procession passes on."

Then there were the ballad singers, who stood in circles at the street corners, impeding the traffic and singing such ballads as "Death and the Lady Margaret's Ghost and Chevy Chase".

Sophie de la Roche noted that the houses in London were not so splendid as those in Paris. "I like this difference" she says "as most of the well-to-do plebeian houses are witness to the fact that England divides up fortune's spoils more equally." If they were witness to anything it was to the rising standards of the lower middle class, and it seems probable that Sophie had never seen the slums, or, if she had, had turned a blind eye to them. "We strolled up and down lovely Oxford Street this evening" she tells us "for some goods look more attractive by artificial light." We all know these goods. "A street" she continues "taking half an hour to cover from end to end, with double rows of brightly shining lamps, in the middle of which stands an equally long row of beautifully lacquered coaches, and on another side of these there is room for two coaches to pass one another and the pavement inlaid with flagstones can stand six people deep and allows one to gaze at the splendidly rich shop fronts in comfort."

Grosley, though he admits that the shops were superior to anything of the kind in Paris, gives a different account of the London streets.

" I have seen " he says " the middle of the street constantly foul with a dirty puddle, where splashings cover those who ride or walk on foot, or in coaches when their windows happen not to be up, and bedaub all the lower parts of such houses as are exposed to it." Baretti, who had the Italian's love of beauty, says that " ugly, hopelessly ugly houses are far too common on every side. The streets are badly paved, filled with mud black as ink and with every kind of filth. It is difficult, unless you are very active upon your feet, to get out of the way of all the horses and carriages which, even if they do not actually touch you, cover your coat with ugly splashes."

The traffic problem existed in those days, and there were many complaints, from Englishmen as well as foreigners, about the congested condition of the London streets, especially those in the City, and the danger of being knocked down and run over.

Pastor Moritz also complained of the filth of the streets. " Nothing in London " he says " makes so disgusting an appearance to a foreigner as the butcher's shops, especially in the environs of the town. Guts and all the nastiness are thrown into the middle of the street and cause an intolerable stench."

The London fog and the general smoke and dirt of the city was much commented upon. Grosley says that if London increased at the rate which seemed probable " the inhabitants must at last bid adieu to all hope of ever seeing the sun ".

Faujas de St. Fond admits that Londoners have to

change their linen twice a day; but he does not think that this fog or smoke affects the health of the inhabitants. "I am very far from thinking" he says "that the city of London is more unhealthy than other cities, because they burn sea coal here. For not only is the contrary proved by experience and a long train of observation; but it is also to be presumed that this immense quantity of fires contributes to its salubrity."

Meister, however, scouts this idea of the healthiness of smoke. "Physicians" he says, with characteristic eighteenth-century scorn of the profession, "may, if they please, tell me that nothing is more wholesome than the sulphurous exhalations which we constantly breathe in London." Those sulphurous exhalations had certainly greatly increased during the century and our practice of burning coal struck foreigners with surprise. De la Rochefoucauld found it at first "most inconvenient. For the first few days I was in England" he says "I was extremely sorry that we had no wood, since it is a long time before one can get warm especially in the feet; but for warming a room coal is much better. Though I found the smell of coal highly disagreeable, I got used to it in a little while, and now that I have been in England for some time, I actually prefer it to wood partly because one is not obliged to attend to it every moment and partly because it gives out more heat." As early as the reign of Charles II Londoners were complaining of the effects of burning sea coal, so called because it was carried by sea and river from north-eastern ports. As the eighteenth century advanced the sooty deposits and the impenetrable fogs increased. There were not many factories in the metropolis so the increase of dirt and soot must have been due to domestic fires, and the fog which became blacker and ever blacker originated in the marshes and undrained land in and around London.

We have all met people whose ancestors shot snipe in Belgrave Square, or who remembered sportsmen who shot them in Sloane Street. It was not until these districts were built over and the Hackney Marshes were drained that the black, impenetrable fogs began to disappear, and " the black rain " of which foreigners complained was no longer a feature of London weather.

It was not only Sophie de la Roche who was enthusiastic about the London shops. " Surely " de la Rochefoucauld says " there can be no other city which has anything so magnificent to show. Everything the merchant possesses is displayed behind windows which are always beautifully clean and the shops are built with a little projection on to the street so that they can be seen from three sides." " The confectioners " Lichtenberg tells us " dazzle your eyes with their candelabra and tickle your nose with their wares ... in these shops hang festoons of Spanish grapes, alternating with pineapples and pyramids of oranges and apples." He saw in a London shop a life-sized bust of Garrick which was priced at two guineas and he begins to complain at once that " things were immoderately dear at least for a German ". He had lived comfortably in Gottingen on £40 a year and London prices shocked him. Grosley comments on a pair of scissors he had seen in a shop window " the branches of which were adorned in filigram mounted in brilliants ". It was, he tells us, " totally deficient in point of taste " and cost fifteen guineas.

De Saussure speaks of a shop " opposite St. Paul's where the most beautiful jewellery in Europe is said to be found. You cannot help admiring the exquisite workmanship, and the riches and curiosities here displayed."

Until the year 1766 London shops had displayed painted signs. These did not necessarily advertise the wares on sale within. There were Roasted Pigs and Spotted Lions, Dogs and Gridirons which had no connection with the contents of the shop. These old signs, interesting though they were, were thought to be a nuisance. They creaked and groaned as they swung aloft and sometimes fell down on the heads of passers-by. In 1766 the signs were removed and when they had gone it was necessary to indicate in some manner what the shop sold. Some kept the emblems of their trade, the barber's pole, the grocer's sugar loaf, the golden arm holding a mallet, which was the sign of the goldsmith. Others had their names and occupations painted above their shops and places of business.

" There is hardly a cobbler " says Moritz " whose name and profession may not be read in large golden characters . . . it is not uncommon to see on doors in one continued succession ' Children educated here, Shoes mended here, Foreign spirituous liquors sold here, and Funerals furnished here.' I am sorry to observe " he adds " that ' Dealer in foreign spirituous liquors ' is by far the most frequent." Shops selling the same sort of wares tended to set up in the same neighbourhood. The booksellers were in Little Britain, chainmakers in St. Paul's Church Yard, fishmongers appropriately on Fish Street Hill, and Paternoster Row was not noted for its books, but for its sempstresses.

" A number of them (streets) are dirty narrow and badly built " de Saussure tells us, " others again are wide and straight, bordered with fine houses. Most of the streets are wonderfully well lighted, for in front of each house hangs a lantern, or a large globe of glass, inside of which is placed a lamp which burns all night. Large houses have two of these lamps suspended outside their doors with iron supports and some have even four."

The superior lighting of the London streets was much

commented on by foreigners. Before 1736 the lighting of the city was entirely a matter for the citizens. Each proprietor whose house fronted on the street was obliged, on moonless nights, to hang out a candle, usually enclosed in a horn lantern, from six o'clock till eleven at night. After this hour the metropolis was in complete darkness, only broken here and there by the gleam of a torch or link. This gloom encouraged every kind of crime, and the Mayor and Corporation at last agreed to levy a rate on householders, and light the city with five thousand oil lamps. It was this illumination which so much impressed the foreigner.

"I think" de Saussure says bitterly "that no cleverer pick-pockets exist than in this country." His snuff-box had been stolen from under a buttoned coat and waistcoat. He goes on to complain of the "surprising number of robbers" in the metropolis. "I am convinced" he says "that, in the thirteen cantons and their allies fewer robbers are caught in a year than are judged in a single London assize." This preponderance of crime had not escaped the notice of the legislature; but the only remedy they could think of was the increase of punishment, and the encouragement of informers and thief takers. These proved to be worse than useless. "It is said" Lichtenberg tells us "that voluptuousness, evil and debauchery have never been so rampant in London as they are at present (1772). Not an evening passes when not only one, but three, four or five robberies are committed by footpads, not to mention burglaries and other crimes. Dozens are hanged and batches of fifty sent off to America, but all this makes no impression on them." The immorality of the city shocked many foreigners. "Every ten yards one is beset even by children of twelve years old" Lichtenberg tells us; "often they seize hold of you in such a fashion of which

I can give you the best notion by the fact that I say nothing about it . . . I cannot understand why no one has tried to put an end to this evil." The authorities had tried. They had established Bridewells where prostitutes were imprisoned and whipped. They had passed laws against solicitation; but it remained a fact that " whole rows " of these unhappy women as Grosley says " accost passengers in broad daylight . . . the list of those who are in any way eminent is publickly cried about the streets. This list which is very numerous points out their places of abode and gives the most circumstantial and exact detail of their features, their stature and the several qualifications for which they are remarkable." Possibly foreigners were more exposed to solicitation than the native; they certainly found the streets of London very dangerous, as Baretti knew to his cost. A prostitute, whose overtures he had rejected, struck him in the face; Baretti returned the blow and became involved with three of her bullies. " I was a Frenchman in their opinion " Baretti says, " which made me apprehensive I must expect no favour or protection, but all outrage and blows." Baretti, though he declared that he did not know how to use his fists, gave one of his assailants such a blow that he afterwards died. He was brought before Sir John Fielding, who committed him to the prison in Tothill Fields, fortunately the best of its kind in London, where the inmates were actually made to wash. Baretti was supported by Johnson, Reynolds and Garrick, who gave evidence at his trial as to his high character. A great point was made by the prosecution that Baretti should have carried a knife. It was according to him " a little fruit knife with a silver blade ", but with it he managed to stab one of the bullies " so that the blood ran down into his boots ". Topham Beauclerk, who was also a friend and supporter, explained to the court that on the Continent it was usual for people to carry knives, as they were not provided at inns or taverns. Baretti was acquitted. There were murmurs about the verdict and the *Gentleman's Magazine* went so far as to suggest that only a foreigner would have got off. This may have been true; it was not the custom for law-abiding Englishmen to carry knives. Baretti, too, was fortunate in his friends. A friendless foreigner might not have fared so well.

It was into this noisy, bustling, crowded city that the traveller ventured, braving pickpockets and cut-throats, bawds and bullies, the mud and filth, the stench and the black rain. It was often difficult for him to find his way and, according to Grosley, the Frenchman, the rabble were " as insolent as can be met with in countries without law or police. Inquire of them your way in the street, if it be upon the right they direct you to the left, or they send you from one of their vulgar comrades to another. The most shocking abuse and ill language make a part of their pleasantry on these occasions. To be assailed in such manner it is not absolutely necessary to be engaged in conversation with them; it is sufficient to pass by them. My French air, notwithstanding the simplicity of my dress, drew upon me, at the corner of every street, a volume of abusive litanies, in the midst of which I slipped on, returning thanks to God that I did not understand English. The constant burthen of these litanies was 'French dog'!" His servant who had followed the crowd to Tyburn fared even worse, and was rescued with difficulty by three French soldiers, deserters from the French guard.

Macky gives a pleasant account of the day as he spent it in London.

" We rise by nine " he says " and those that frequent great men's levées, find entertainment at them till eleven, or as in Holland, we go to tea tables. About twelve the beau monde assembles in several chocolate and coffee houses, the best of which are the Cocoa Tree and White's Chocolate House, Mrs. Rochford's and the British Coffee House. We are carried to these places in chairs (or sedans) which are here very cheap, a guinea a week or a shilling per hour, and your chairmen serve you for porters and run your errands. If it be fine weather we take a turn in the park till two, when we go to dinner, and if it be dirty you are entertained at picquet or basset at White's or you may talk politics at the Smyrna or the St. James's . . . at two we generally go to dinner. The general way here is to make up a party at the Coffee House to go dine at a tavern where we sit till six when we go to the play except you are invited to the table of some great man, where strangers are always courted and nobly entertained . . . or, if you like rather the company of ladies, there are assemblies at most of the people of qualities' houses."

The sedan chairs were a feature of English town life. They could, as Macky says, be hired by the week or picked up at a stand in the street like a hackney coach. The passenger was set down at the door of the house he wished to visit; on wet and foggy nights, he could be carried inside and put down in the hall. If the bearers kept in step the motion was pleasant, far better than that of a hackney coach jolting over the uneven stones of the London streets. They were useful for visiting the numerous sights which the foreigner was anxious to see. De la Rochefoucauld thinks " that the conduct of an Englishman's day in London leaves little time for work ". He was, of course, speaking of the life of the upper classes. He tells us how the Englishman " gets up at ten or eleven and has breakfast (always with tea). He then " he continues " makes a tour of the town for about four hours until 5 o'clock, which is the dinner hour, at nine he meets in a tavern or a club and there the night is passed in play or drink ; that is precisely how the day is spent."

Early in the century Zetzner saw in progress the re-building of St. Paul's Cathedral after the great fire. On this, he tells us, a thousand workmen were employed daily. Most travellers admired St. Paul's, " a fine and elegant imitation of St. Peter's church in Rome ", and de Saussure describes it as " the most truly magnificent in all London and England ". Meister admired Westminster Abbey and called it " that remarkable specimen of Gothic architecture ". Other travellers were less enthusiastic. " This structure " Grosley says, speaking of Henry VII's chapel, " resembles that goddess whom an unskilled artist represented in most gorgeous apparel because he could not give her an elegant shape. The English, he thought, " had a rambling taste " but he found much to admire in Walpole's villa at Twickenham. The Abbey was certainly greatly neglected. The monuments were broken and scribbled over. An Italian cardinal had knocked off a piece of the coronation stone and taken it away with him, and Von Politz thought that the custodian would " have sold the whole stone for a guinea ".

Walpole had described the neglected state of the Abbey and declared that " monuments tumble upon one's head through their neglect as one of them did and killed a man at Lady Elizabeth Percy's funeral ".

The Houses of Parliament were not, Moritz tells us, open to the public. Visitors could be introduced only by a member. He found, however, that the price of a bottle of wine, which was two shillings in those halcyon days, served as well as any introduction. " It is not uncommon " he says " to see a member lying stretched

LONDON FROM BLACKFRIARS BRIDGE

Drawn by L. Clennell *Engraved by W. B. Cooke*

out on one of the benches while others are debating. Some crack nuts, others eat oranges or whatever else is in season. The many rude things which the members said to each other struck me much. It is astonishing with what violence and even rudeness they push and jostle each other. Some members bring their sons whilst quite little boys and carry them to their seats along with themselves." The Houses of Parliament were, of course, the old buildings which were destroyed by fire in the following century. They were large gloomy chambers, the House of Commons being particularly funereal. Iron pillars with gilded Corinthian capitals supported the galleries of the Lower House. These had been erected by Sir Christopher Wren in the reign of Queen Anne when he had been called in to repair and restore the chamber. Until that date the walls had been hung with the tapestries which Queen Elizabeth had ordered to commemorate the defeat of the Armada, one of which depicted Sir Richard Grenville's ship *The Revenge* fighting against the ships of Spain. Unfortunately most of these priceless hangings were swept away to make room for Wren's galleries. The House of Lords was less gloomy than the Commons. Here the very uncomfortable wooden benches, with which both chambers were furnished, had been painted crimson, the hangings of the throne were of the same colour and the old tapestries remained. Fine, gilt candelabra hung in both chambers. Kielmansegg also complained of the difficulty he experienced in getting into the House of Commons, that he had had to stand from half-past two to eight o'clock and could hardly use his arms and legs next day. " Still " he says, " I should be wrong if I were to say that I had found the time tedious." He had heard some very fine orators, including Pitt, " one of the most powerful speakers of our time ", and he adds that " absolute silence reigns in the whole House ". Francesco de Miranda, the Venezuelan patriot who was in England at the close of the century, describes the debates in the House of Commons as " really a sublime school of politics and legislation for the man of application ". Von Uffenbach, who apparently visited St. Stephen's when the members were not sitting, complained that the great expectations he had formed " are monstrously disappointed. The woolsack " he adds " is very hard to sit on."

The Tower was another sight which attracted many visitors. Von Uffenbach was enthusiastic about the Tower. " There are " he says " such precious things here, crowns, jewels that I cannot sufficiently express my amazement. The most remarkable thing is that the armour of the old Kings of England is seen on full sized, wooden figures. The most notable is King Henry VIII, whose armour is of prodigious size. The head piece, like the stomach piece and breeches, is lined with velvet. For a jest countless pins have been stuck into this velvet, and any young person, particularly females, who come here, are presented with one because they are supposed to be a charm against impotence and barrenness."

The average sightseer was generally less interested in crowns and jewels and Henry VIII's armour than in the Tower Menagerie. De Saussure dismisses the relics of the past by saying that to see all these " would take you several days, and would be to your cost ". He describes the menagerie as " a small, rather dirty place containing ten lions, one panther, two tigers and four leopards. Also what the keeper calls a tiger man, a very big monkey wide striped like a tiger. We were told " he adds " that this animal is very intelligent, and I will give you proof of this. One day the poor beast being ill, a little wine was given it, which seemed to do it good. The rogue found it excellent and having remarked that no wine was given him unless he were ill he feigned sickness two or three times in order to receive the coveted remedy. The keeper, we are told, discovered this and beat the poor creature soundly."

Sophie de la Roche pities the unhappy creatures in their miserable, cramped quarters, especially the eagles fastened by thongs to the beams. It made her as unhappy, she says, as if she had seen " fine young men, born with good intellect condemned to low servile work".

Pity for caged animals was, however, even more rare in the eighteenth century than it is in these days. Visitors flocked to the Tower and to the other menageries in London.

. Count Kielmansegg tells us that near Westminster Bridge he found " a quantity of outlandish animals such as a large, white-haired water animal which we took to be a sea bear from Greenland, a camel and a quantity of monkeys, eagles, civet cats, etc."

Englishmen complained of the difficulties they met with on trying to visit the British Museum. At one time admission could only be obtained by ticket for which application had to be made to the Museum porter, with a statement of " names, condition and residence with the day and hour when they desire to visit the house ". Not more than ten tickets were issued for any one hour and there were other tiresome and deterring regulations. Perhaps foreigners were more used to regimentation in their own countries. Count Kielmansegg certainly did not complain about having to obtain a ticket. What he noted with approbation in this country " where a man's hand was always in his pocket ", was the fact that " no servant or warder etc. is allowed to receive a penny under penalty of dismissal ". He adds that the maintenance and heating of the museum cost £8,000 a year, a very large sum in those days. Moritz, however, talks about "venal praters who ten times a day repeat the same dull lesson they have got by heart", and complains that he was rushed through the museum and only saw glass cases and shelves and had a hasty view of the library. De la Rochefoucauld thought that the collections could not compare with those in France, but he admired the public spirit of the English. "A considerable portion of the exhibits" he says "has been voluntarily given and every day new legacies are recorded."

Meister speaks with enthusiasm of the Leverian Museum, and this was indeed considered to be better arranged and more interesting than the British Museum. It comprised the collections of Sir Ashton Lever and was housed for a time in Leicester House, Leicester Square, which had once been "the pouting place of princes". It had, Meister says, "the best collection of birds ever exhibited, with a collection of uncommon articles brought from the several places discovered by Captain Cook, consisting of dresses, arms, idols and utensils of every kind, together with the coat of mail which Cromwell wore when he defeated the royal army". Baron Dimsdale, who had seen the museums of Moscow, St. Petersburg, Dresden and Paris, declared that the whole of these collections could not be compared with the Leverian Museum. It was open freely every day to anyone who cared to enter and there were no tiresome restrictions.

Besides the ordinary everyday sights there were special occasions and of these perhaps the chief was the Lord Mayor's procession on the 9th of November. Zetzner tells us how he went to this, and saw three men, entirely naked and looking like savages, running through the streets. They had vowed that they would never wear coat or shirt till James II had been restored to the throne.

LORD MAYOR'S DAY

"They assure me that they are persons of high rank" Zetzner adds. When he came near the route of the procession he was nearly crushed to death and was carried by the crowd for several minutes. Fearing that he "would be reduced to marmalade" he got out of the throng and returned home, having seen nothing more interesting than the three naked men. Count Kielmansegg was more enterprising. He declined to pay one or two guineas for a seat on the roof or on an unsafe stand, but contrived to catch glimpses of the show from the crowd. "The cheering for Pitt" he tells us "nearly exceeded that for the King and Queen." He had some difficulty in moving on as the people hung on to his carriage and horses.

"At these times" de Saussure tells us, speaking of the Lord Mayor's Day, "it is almost dangerous for an honest man, and more particularly for a foreigner, if at all well dressed, to walk the streets, for he runs a great risk of being insulted by the vulgar populace which is the most cursed brood in existence. He is sure of not only being jeered at and being bespattered with mud, but as likely as not dead dogs and cats will be thrown at him, for the mob makes a provision beforehand of these play-things, so that they may amuse themselves with them on the great day." De Saussure saw the Lord Mayor on the day of his investiture go in his barge from the City to Westminster. "The Lord Mayor's barge is magnificent" he says; "it is enriched with gilding, carving and delicate paintings, it is decked with banners, streamers and flags, and is manned by forty oarsmen all wearing a bright hued livery and caps of black velvet. The other barges are handsomely decorated likewise, one of them having a band of music on board."

This voyage from the City of Westminster was preliminary to the Lord Mayor's Show. The Lord Mayor having gone to Guildhall where he was met by the outgoing Lord Mayor, arrayed himself in his robes. He then proceeded to the Three Cranes Wharf accompanied by javelin men, footmarshals, livery men of the City companies and their pensioners in bright coloured gowns and caps. The Lord Mayor's barge, followed by others carrying the attendant company, was rowed to Westminster, where at New Palace Stairs they disembarked. The javelin men made a lane, a necessary precaution in earlier times, and the Lord Mayor passed through it to Westminster Hall, where he took the necessary oaths and left a handsome sum of money to be distributed among the poor.

Queen Elizabeth had still a place in the affections and memories of many Englishmen, and her birthday was observed with processions, bonfires and the burning of unpopular effigies. To the mob it was another excuse for violence, robbery and drunkenness. "The last birthday" a foreign traveller writes "was kept with great solemnity. I saw the procession of the Pope, the devil and the Chevalier de St. George on that night performed in great order, as also their being burnt at the expense of the Hanover Club at Charing Cross."

May Day was observed in London as the chimney-sweep's festival, and also as a holiday for milkmaids. De Saussure saw the milkmaids dancing a jig in the Strand "One of these maidens" he says "carried a trophy of different pieces of crockery and tinsel on her head; she was accompanied by young men playing the fiddle and they stopped and danced before various houses, from which they received food and money." This trophy was known as the milkmaid's garland, and though de Saussure speaks of it contemptuously as crockery and tinsel, it usually consisted of a frame in the shape of a pyramid, hung round with pewter and silver dishes. The plate, which was often valuable, had been borrowed from pawnbrokers, and the structure was not usually carried on the head, it was born through the streets on a hand-bier, sometimes in the shape of a horse. The company stopped only at the houses of customers, where they were regaled as de Saussure describes.

London parks seem to have impressed the foreigner. " This place " says de Saussure, speaking of the Mall, " is no longer used for the game (pall-mall) but is a promenade and every spring it is bestrewn with tiny sea shells which are then crushed by means of a heavy roller. Deer and roe-deer are so tame that they eat out of your hand, and there is little danger of being attacked in the neighbourhood of the palace, for should the offender be taken up in any of these privileged parts, the laws would condemn him to lose his hand." Von Uffenbach also mentions the red deer and speaks of the cows in St. James's Park, or the May Park as he calls it. He does not tell us if he had a glass of milk warm from the cow which many visitors to the Park were in the habit of drinking. He saw a man bearing a cask walking among the carriages and sprinkling the dusty roads with water. This was a variant of the water cart, which even then was to be seen in London streets. Hyde Park was surrounded by a brick wall and like St. James's was well stocked with deer. Macky counted three hundred coaches in succession going round the Ring.

" Nothing is more beautiful than the road from London to Kensington crossing Hyde Park " de Saussure tells us. Kensington Gardens, as von Uffenbach says, had " sun boxes which could be turned round on pivots ", a form of summer-house, which has been re-invented in our own day. These gardens could be entered only by ticket, and the parks, though they were declared open to the public, admitted only well-dressed persons, and on weekdays were supposed to be the close preserve of the upper classes. Here ladies, who would be escorted by male relatives or footmen while walking the dangerous London streets, might go alone as it was supposed that they would meet no one but their friends and other persons of their own class. It was the sole taste of liberty which most of them ever enjoyed, and there were those who made the best of it. Many women, during the earlier years of the century, wore masks at the theatre or other public places, and protected by these, some would talk to anyone they met.

Besides the sights of London which we have described there were others of a repulsive kind. Count Kielmansegg went to Tyburn to see a man hanged " à l'anglais ". De Saussure visited Bridewell, where he saw " thirty or forty robbers, pickpockets, etc. occupied in beating flax. Each of those unfortunate wretches was seated in front of a large block of wood on which he beat the flax with a large heavy mallet. On one side of the room were the men, on the other the women and between the lines walked an inspector or Captain Whip'em. This man had a surly, repulsive countenance ; he held a long cane in his hand about the thickness of my little finger and whenever one of these ladies was fatigued or ceased working he would rap her on the arms and in no gentle fashion. One young girl of fifteen and extremely beautiful said she was there ' because of my tender heart '. She had helped some friend to steal and was sent to Bridewell for two weeks. She had been there three as she could not afford the crown garnish money." This was a sum payable to the turnkey before a prisoner could be liberated. De Saussure tells us that the friend, who was with him, was so shocked and indignant that he paid the five shillings for the girl's release.

CHAPTER 6

Amusements and Sports

THE English theatre had a great fascination for foreigners. Many of them give long accounts of the plays they witnessed and of the actors and actresses.

The chief and indeed, for many years, the only two licensed theatres in London, besides the Opera House in the Haymarket, were Drury Lane and Covent Garden. Other plays, unlicensed by the Lord Chamberlain, were performed in taverns, in Assembly Rooms or even in private houses. Plays in these places would be termed rehearsals and the tickets for them could be bought at some neighbouring shop or inn.

" There are three very noble theatres here " says Macky ; " that of the opera at the end of Pall Mall or the Haymarket is the finest I ever saw . . . the parterre, commonly called the pit containing the gentlemen on benches, and on the first stage of boxes it is the ladies of quality, in the second the citizens wives and daughters and in the third the common people and footmen." Seats in this upper gallery cost a shilling and the footmen who sat there had been at the theatre from the time it opened keeping seats in the boxes until their mistresses arrived. They did not dare look out from these or they would have been pelted with rotten oranges. Foreigners noted with surprised disapprobation the uproar that was permitted in the shilling seats. When an Englishman had paid that sum he considered himself the equal, if not the superior, of the pit and boxes. He would even throw glasses of water on the heads of the gentlemen beneath him. Kielmansegg found that the audience would not wait even for the King, and insisted upon the performance beginning. When he arrived the gallery booed and hissed and shouted " lower lower " as they did not consider his bow sufficiently pronounced. Kielmansegg saw the Queen Dowager make one of the young princes bow lower by forcibly pushing his head forward. The King looked at his watch and shook his head, which placated the gallery, who then broke out into cheers. In no other country in the world could there have been such a scene. Rude and boorish though such conduct was, it typified the English sense of independence and equality, the " Jack's as good as his master " tradition which was still to be found among what were then called the lower orders. The gallery would also, when opportunity offered, express its opinion of any unpopular person. Von Uffenbach tells us how he went to see *The Recruiting Officer* and how in one of the intervals a troop of soldiers came on the stage singing a song of the army in Flanders about the Duke of Marlborough. It praised Prince Eugene, but the Duke was much censured for his meanness. This song was sung with enthusiasm by the audience, " Who " von Uffenbach tells us " bandied about monstrous insults although Marlborough's daughter, the Duchess of Montagu, was herself at the play, and was so greatly shamed that she was covered with blushes." As Dr. Johnson wrote of Garrick :

> The dramas laws, the drama patrons give,
> For we that live to please must please to live.

Sometimes the gallery proceeded to violence if anything happened to displease it. Casanova describes how the audience wrecked Drury Lane because a piece had been substituted for the one advertised. On another occasion, when this had occurred, Garrick appeared before the curtain to apologize. "A voice from the pit shouted ' on your knees ', a thousand voices took up the cry ' on your knees '. Roscius was obliged to kneel and ask forgiveness. Then came a thunder of applause and everything was over."

" In this island " says Lichtenberg " at the time that the additional tax was laid upon porter the King's ears were saluted in the theatre with all the indecent freedom of expression which the utmost bitterness of resentment could suggest to a haughty people." It may seem to us extraordinary that in an age when the divine right of kings was still being preached and the power of the monarch was very great, such scenes could take place. One cannot imagine them occurring under the last of the Stuarts. Something of the glamour and romance of kings had departed or perhaps was being slowly extinguished at St. Germains. The Whigs, backed by a majority of the people, had brought over the Hanoverians and could, if they pleased, send them packing. They were now their servants and as such were beginning to bow to their will.

When Zetzner went to the theatre in 1700, he was horrified at the price of seats. As much as 12*s.* was asked for a side box, and 10*s.* for one facing the stage, the pit was 2*s.* 6*d.* and the gallery 1*s.* It is interesting to notice that these prices for pit and gallery were the same in the earlier years of this century.

There were long intervals between the acts. It took longer to shift scenery in those days and the audience filled in the time by taking refreshment. Women walked about the house selling apples and oranges, beer and strong waters were passed round. It was possible, too, to obtain more substantial provisions. Casanova gave the four friends, who accompanied him, a fine meal consisting of oysters, hare, larks, ortolans, truffles and sweetmeats with champagne and liqueurs. According to him this repast cost ten guineas; but Casanova's statements about money, as about other things, are frequently exaggerated.

The comments of foreign travellers about our plays and actors differ widely and are interesting. The French, though they liked our comedies and farces, considered our tragedies coarse and bloodthirsty and complained that we had no great playwrights. Macky, however, praises our historical plays and says that " One Shakespeare, who lived in the last century, laid down a masterly foundation for this in his excellent plays, and the late Mr. Addison hath improved that taste in his admirable *Cato*."

Grosley on the other hand was distinctly shocked " At the representations of *Macbeth*, *Richard III*, *King Lear* and other pieces of Shakespeare which I happened to be a spectator of, whatever the most barbarous cruelty and the most refined wickedness can possibly conceive is presented to view."

Meister merely complains that Shakespeare had been so altered and cut about that " not one of his pieces is represented on the stage as he wrote it. There are some so disguised as not to be discoverable for his writing."

This was indeed the truth. Even Garrick did not venture to present the Bard in his original form. An age which had accepted Wycherley now drew the line at the grossness of Shakespeare. Kemble wished to eliminate the ghost from *Macbeth*, but Meister tells us that he was afraid to do it as the gallery would have stopped the performance and called out for the ghost.

" None of his " (Shakespeare's) " tragedies " Meister

continues " have caused so many tears to be shed as I have seen drop at the representation of *Jane Shore*, *Venice Preserved*, *the Grecian Daughters* or *the Gamester*. . . . Poets of talent perhaps far inferior to his have better understood the secret of touching our feelings or beguiling us of our tears."

Count Kielmansegg dismisses the Tragedy of *Richard III*, Cibber's version, as " quite in the English tragic style, very bloody". He also saw *Henry VIII* and *King Lear*. The latter he considered " very much in the style of the old English plays . . . in which most of the characters go mad, get blind or die ". Voltaire described Shakespeare's tragedies as " monstrous farces ", but thought that if he had lived in Addison's day he " might have written a play as good as *Cato* ".

Pastor Moritz on the other hand declared that Shakespeare was the greatest genius nature ever produced, and Meister said that " *Macbeth* is productive of the greatest degree of wonder and astonishment ". On the whole, however, foreigners did not think much of Shakespeare. Frenchmen compared him unfavourably with Corneille and Racine, and Germans preferred some of their own turgid dramatists, whose names are now forgotten.

As for lighter plays they found it " difficult to reconcile the general moral conduct for which these people are renowned with the great immorality and indecency of their comedies ". They were particularly shocked by *The Beggar's Opera*, but this play had profoundly shocked the English themselves. De Saussure did not think it " at all refined or witty ". On the whole he preferred the pantomime which Rich produced at a cost of £4,000. This was *Orpheus in the Lower Regions*. " There was a serpent " de Saussure tells us " of enormous size ; covered all over with green and gold scales ; his eyes shine like fire and he wriggles about the theatre with head upraised, making an awful, but very natural hissing noise. This so frightened a grenadier stationed near the stage, that he dropped his musket, drew his sword and tried to kill the reptile."

When Voltaire came to England he was delighted to find the status of actors and actresses very different from what it was in France. There the body of Adrienne Lecouvreur had been thrown out upon a Paris dunghill, here in London Nance Oldfield was laid to rest in Westminster Abbey, with peers for her pall-bearers. The enthusiasm for great actors and actresses was widespread. There was, of course, the Puritan element which regarded the theatre as the abode of iniquity and the performers as rogues and vagabonds. In the early days of the century plays were often so gross that reputable women, if they went to the theatre at all, went there masked. Public taste improved, however, and demanded a certain amount of decency on the stage. When Sheridan adapted Vanbrugh's comedy *The Relapse* he omitted most of his grossness with possibly some of his wit and the *Trip to Scarborough* offended no one. Ladies no longer wore masks at the theatre; according to Zetzner the only women to do this were prostitutes; a clergyman even had been known to go there, though he did not go " openly in his habit " as Swift described it. Garrick was received everywhere, and Mrs. Siddons was adored.

Sophie de la Roche tells us how a gentleman at a party had said that he paid Mrs. Siddons a visit and found her " at her sick child's cot, rocking it with her foot, and holding another at her breast with her rôle in her hand." The company was so affected by this tale " that " says Sophie " it wants to publish an engraved portrait of this estimable lady in this position without alteration."

The foreigner had very little but praise for the great English actors. Lichtenberg gives a detailed and laudatory account of Garrick and tells us that " he moves to and fro among the players like a man among marionettes". Mrs. Barry he considers to be the only English actress who could compare with him. Speaking of her performance as Cordelia, he says " it still provides a feast for my imagination, which will live in my memory till my dying day". " Having seen the English Melpomene (Mrs. Siddons) I think " Meister says " I have seen for the first time the tragic muse in all the dignity of the buskin, with all the majesty of her sceptre, and encircled with all her fascinating charms. . . . I saw Lady Macbeth or Calista or Belvedera or Jane Shore or Volumnia by turns before me, I heard them speak without noticing their language whether mine or their own . . . they spoke a language which my heart perfectly understood."

He was not so enthusiastic about other English actresses. Mrs. Pope he describes as " a precise old woman ", Mrs. Powell wanted feeling and dignity, Mrs. Elston he admits was young and handsome, " but her talents ", he adds unkindly, " are younger than her face and perhaps may ever continue so ". Mrs. Jordan " possessed a deal of witchcraft, enough to fascinate the Duke of Clarence ".

Count Kielmansegg, however, praises the good all-round quality of English acting. " In general " he says " the English theatre has the advantage of a good caste for every piece and the faces of the actors look as if they were cut out for the parts they represent."

If London provided few theatres, there were other entertainments. First and foremost there were the pleasure gardens. Taverns and inns on the outskirts of the town had their gardens with lawns and ornamental shrubs. Many had ponds and fountains, some had dancing on the grass or in an adjacent ballroom, or bands playing music among the trees. The largest and most famous of these gardens were those of Ranelagh and Vauxhall, and foreigners were generally taken to see them. Grosley thought that these were " finer in appearance than the Houses of Parliament, Courts of Justice or the King's Palace ". Of Ranelagh he says, " Imagine to yourself the salon, amphitheatre and boxes all fitted with company and on the ground floor a multitude of persons walking in every direction, the murmurings of the crowd drowned by a continuous symphony, the whole illuminated with a milder gleam than that of the day. There were few objects more striking."

This salon was the Rotunda where concerts and ridottos were held. The charge for the ridottos, which were assemblies for dancing and music, was a guinea; but the entrance to the Gardens was only a shilling, or half a crown if refreshments were included. Count Kielmansegg, who was always talking about prices and comparing ours unfavourably with those of the Continent, was really pleased about this. You could consume as much tea and bread and butter as you liked, he said. He noted, too, with equal surprise and less approval, that everyone was equal at Ranelagh and Vauxhall, no distinction was made between classes and he had not got to take off his hat to the Duke of York when he passed him. Of Vauxhall he says, " The garden " (he visited it by day) " must be a wonderful sight when the greater part of it is lighted up with nearly 1,500 glass lamps. At one end of an avenue, when a curtain is withdrawn, a landscape is to be seen, illuminated by hidden lamps, the principal feature being a miller's house with an artificial cascade, you fancy that you see water driving the mill and that you hear the rush of it, though in reality there is none. It is arranged just as these things are arranged in theatres and pantomimes."

Moritz saw there " A picture of the surrender of a besieged city, which affects you so much that you even shed tears ". He describes Ranelagh Gardens, which were the more fashionable of the two, as " poor and mean looking and ill lighted " but is enthusiastic about the Rotunda, " the splendour and beauty of which surpassed everything of the kind I had ever seen before. I felt pretty nearly the same sensations that I remember to have felt when in early youth I first read the *Fairy Tales*." The company, he tells us, was more select than at Vauxhall, the expense " nothing near so great, and no one without silk stockings ", which must have been very gratifying.

According to Mme de Bocage such places of amusement as Ranelagh and Vauxhall were unknown in France. " There are here " she says " entertainments of which we have no idea. I do not mean horse-races, cock-fights or combats of prize-fighters ; I leave it to men to describe those shocking amusements, and shall dwell upon more pleasing subjects, such as the gardens of Vauxhall which are to be seen upon the delightful banks of the Thames . . . Persons of all ranks and ages come in a negligent dress from all quarters to soothe their cares by innocent amusement. The French look upon it as a phenomenon that there should be so much order and so profound a silence in the midst of such a multitude whilst, with us, the smallest assembly occasions a stunning noise."

On Ranelagh where " winter passed unnoticed owing to the furnace with four fronts the heat of which penetrated without being excessive ", Mme de Bocage breaks into verse :

> Muse, charmer of my leisure hours,
> Paint to the French those blissful bowers
> Where joy and peace and gay desire
> In just proportions still conspire
> And, more to elevate each heart
> To nature add the charms of art
> A thousand instruments around
> In jocund concert there resound
> And fast beside a limpid stream
> Unnumbered lamps diffuse a gleam
> And though a thousand storms arise
> With varied pleasure feast our eyes
> To paint to each succeeding race
> The charms of this delightful place
> Thy architecture now displays
> The grandeur of Rome's ancient days
>
> . . . .
>
> To all the gifts this land affords
> Adds China tea to crown their boards.

Mrs. Cornelys kept what seems to have been a glorified night club at her house in Soho Square and foreigners, who had a taste for that sort of thing, often went there. She was said to have had a turnover of £24,000 but her expenses were enormous. Casanova went to one of her assemblies and describes her large hall as being magnificent and seating 400 people. There was a dance which lasted all night, and " the waste and prodigality were worthy of a prince's palace ".

The receipts for this entertainment were, Casanova tells us, as much as 1,200 guineas, but Theresa's prosperity was short lived. Scandals were whispered about her, and what was more detrimental, the Pantheon was opened and proved a greater attraction. Mrs. Cornelys got into debt, was imprisoned in the Fleet and finally came down to selling asses' milk in Knightsbridge.

A more disreputable place of entertainment was the Royal Diversion or Folly. This was a building on the banks of the Thames, half tavern, half brothel, where such exhibitions as sword-dancing might be witnessed. " All manner of wine can be drunk here " von Uffenbach tells us, " but it sells prodigious dear." He goes on to describe a female sword-dancer who " took two sharp swords between her breasts, two in her eyes and three with the points of her mouth, holding them with her teeth. She twirled round with great rapidity on a barrel for a good half hour. This is a wild and dangerous English fashion of diversion " he adds. Von Uffenbach had a discreet and frugal mind; de Saussure, who does not boggle about the expense, goes into more detail. " The first floor " (of the Folly) he tells us " consists of a large room in which you find a band of musicians and water nymphs eating and drinking with Tritons and other sea divinities, who go and visit them. On the second floor are a few small apartments where the nymphs, or more properly the syrens tired of the world retire, and, for fear of being lonely, invite a friend to amuse them."

On the opposite side of the river were Cuper's Gardens. These had been started by Boydell Cuper who was gardener to Lord Arundel, and the name became corrupted into Cupid's Gardens as more appropriate. They occupied much the same site as that now designed for the Festival of Britain. Here, von Uffenbach tells us, there were " disgraceful goings on. Near it is a tavern where men drink and find occasion for the devil's own work." Disgusted with these entertainments he went to see a Scotsman who broke glasses by shouting at them, which was at least a harmless amusement, if rather tame. De Saussure saw two women fighting with two-handled swords, which so revolted him that he went hastily away, regretting the half-crown he had paid for admission and resolving never to go to such an entertainment again. He thought that cock-fighting was " much more diverting ". " Some of the fighting cocks " he tells us " are celebrated and have pedigrees like gentlemen of good family, some of them being worth five or six guineas. I am told that when transported to France they degenerate and their strength and courage disappear, and they become like ordinary cocks. . . . Would you believe it at this place (the Whitehall Cockpit) several hundred pounds are sometimes lost and won." As de Saussure suggests the principal interest in cock-fighting was the betting. Von Uffenbach tells us how " an ostler in an apron often wins several guineas from a lord " and he goes on to describe how " if a man has made a bet and cannot pay, he is made to sit in a basket fastened to the ceiling and is drawn up in it amidst peals of laughter. This is a sport " he says " peculiar to the English which appears to foreigners very foolish."

In spite of this von Uffenbach goes on to tell us that " a special building has been made for it near Gray's Inn ", and that " the cocks are fed on special globules and on strong wine and sack so that they are very expensive to keep ". After visiting the cockpit von Uffenbach goes to see a bull-baiting. He gives a revolting description of this horrible affair and then says, " Thus concluded this truly English sport, which vastly delights this nation but to me seems nothing very special."

The Frenchman, de Saussure, was less brutal in his tastes. Though he tolerated cock-fighting, he disliked the throwing at cocks which took place on Shrove Tuesday. This sport was condemned by some Englishmen, but Londoners flocked to the Dog and Duck or

Hockley-in-the-Hole at Clerkenwell whenever it was advertised.

Von Uffenbach went to Hockley-in-the-Hole but this was to see " a fight with wooden swords between an Englishman and a Moor ". He did not seem to have enjoyed it. The common people on the ground floor tried to climb up into the gallery and when they were prevented " they cast up such monstrous showers of stones, sticks and filth and this with no respect of persons ... they behaved like madmen and things looked very ugly ". He was not reassured by being told that people had been killed in the place, or had died from the wounds they had received.

" Boxing matches " Meister tells us " are conducted with all the noble generosity of the ages of chivalry. The antagonists are sure to meet with seconds who encourage and advise them, affording them every assistance they can have need of. The antagonist who has received a fall in the contest is never suffered to be attacked whilst lying on the ground. If either combatant is under the necessity of recovering his breath a knee is offered him as a seat, one man is employed in wiping off the dirt and sweat, whilst another presents drink to strengthen and refresh him." As a matter of fact, boxing in those days, before there were any Queensberry Rules, was generally a brutal sport. Men fought with their bare fists, contests dragged on for hours, and many of the professional boxers, or bruisers as they were called, had no notion of fair play. Betting was heavy and led to a further degradation of the sport.

Casanova tells us that at one prize-fight a man was lying at the point of death. A surgeon was present and was ready to bleed him, and, though one might have thought that he had lost enough blood already, that, from the point of view of eighteenth-century surgery, was the correct thing to do. Casanova very naturally asked why it was not done. The friend who was with him explained that two men had betted twenty guineas on the prize-fighter's death or recovery, and that the man who had betted on his death would not allow the surgeon to proceed. Casanova takes this horror very coolly. " The English are very strange in their betting proclivities " is his only comment.

Of football, the national game of the present day, very little is said. De Saussure describes " a score of rascals in the street kicking at a ball, and they will break panes of glass and smash the windows of coaches, and also knock you down without the smallest compunction; on the contrary they will roar with laughter ".

No wonder that Strutt in his *Book of Sports and Pasttimes* says that football " seems to have fallen into disrepute ". Cricket de Saussure will not attempt to describe. " It is too complicated " he says.

The circus, which as all lovers of animals must regret, is still with us, was very popular in the eighteenth century. There had, for long, been exhibitions of wild beasts and performing animals; but the first London circus was set up by Philip Astley near Westminster Bridge towards the end of the century. Sophie de la Roche tells us that " children from seven to twelve ride there and perform a hundred and one tricks. The scenes with these children grieved me."

Sophie had a tender heart. No Englishmen grieved about performing children, and few concerned themselves with the misery of those employed in mill and mine; but even Sophie who had pitied the beasts in the Tower does not grieve about the performing animals. With a few exceptions the eighteenth century was callous as regards the suffering of the beasts.

Von Uffenbach, who carped at most things English,

was not even pleased with Mrs. Salmon's Wax Works, though they were much admired by Londoners. This show was in Fleet Street near the entrance to the Temple. Figures of a beef-eater and a match woman were placed on either side of the door as attractions, and having paid the fee of sixpence, visitors would go through the toy-shop on the ground floor and up to the candle-lit rooms on the first floor. There were, von Uffenbach tells us, " six rooms full of all kinds of wax figures, mostly life size and representing ancient tales, especially English ones ... her work is tolerable, though Frau Braunin in Frankfort makes much more elegant work". He dismisses the show in very few words, and possibly at the date, when he visited London, it was not particularly good. Later in the century, we are told that it was crowded with waxworks. There were George III and Queen Charlotte, the Prince of Wales, General Wolfe and Dr. Johnson, John Wilkes with a cracked nose, Whitefield beside a bevy of Bishops, and Wesley apparently conversing with Dick Turpin. There were also models of shepherds and shepherdesses with their lambs and goats and a man-of-war in wax upon a sea of glass.

De la Rochefoucauld gives us an account of racing and especially of the horses which he admired so much. " These people " he says, speaking of race-horse owners, " have from time immemorial taken the greatest pride in the breeding of their horses; they treasure their pedigrees more jealously than their own, and they never cross their breeds. In fact their horses have always been recognized as the finest in the world."

He confesses that he does not understand the English system of betting. It was highly complicated, " and to acquire all this knowledge is so difficult " he says " that those Englishmen who have mastered the various points regard it as quite extraordinary that Mr. Fox should have been able, in five weeks of intensive study, to grasp it's intricacies. In fact they consider it to be evidence of the mastery of his genius."

"Racing debts" de la Rochefoucauld tells us, were nearly always paid and in case of a defaulter it was "the only occasion on which you may give yourself the pleasure of dealing faithfully with a man with the help of a stick or a whip; you can also set your groom on his track, which gives the groom much satisfaction."

Baretti tells us how he stayed at a town called Visbecohie which was possibly Wisbech. Here, after being bored by his host, "a melancholy man and not in the least lively", and his mother, "who cares for nothing but staying in her room and reading the Bible", Baretti discovered that there were races somewhere in the neighbourhood. He had never seen a horse-race before and he describes how the horses ran three times round the course, a distance of three miles in less than six minutes which seems to have been extraordinary good going.

"When the first race is over" he says "the noble animals have an hour's rest, and a number of men set to work to rub them down and dry them thoroughly and quickly, so that they can run again and then a third time after the lapse of an hour, and the horse which has shown the best legs wins, and its owner pockets the money, while the others scratch their heads and curse their luck." When the races were over, the company adjourned to the inn where they were staying and changed into their best clothes.

"About an hour after sunset" Baretti says "we go to the ball, which takes place in a public hall, ladies being admitted free, and then they begin by dancing minuets just as we do at public balls at home. After this they throw themselves wildly into the country dances, which fire the blood of men and women alike. When they are tired out with dancing, supper, which has been prepared in another large room, is announced. Everyone hastens to sit down at a huge table made by placing a number of small tables of the same size close together. The men take their places in a long row on one side, and the ladies on the other, each man facing his own partner. Some good clergyman, or if there is none present, some important person in the neighbourhood asks a blessing on the food in a short grace, everyone standing and saying Amen, after which there is eating and drinking and laughing and joking of all kinds; but decency and good manners everywhere prevail, and the man who ventured to give the slightest offence to the ladies by a doubtful allusion or a questionable story, as is so common in that disreputable Venice of ours, would be looked upon as the last of flesh. When this delightful supper is over, the bill is divided, each gentleman paying his share. Then we go back and dance or watch the dancing, and not till dawn peeps out of her window in the east do we break up and go home."

CHAPTER 7

Education, Arts and the Universities

SOME foreigners came to England purely on business and a few for pleasure; but many of these showed a passing interest in intellectual things and there were a few scholars who came to study. These latter were usually well received. The Royal Society made Benjamin Franklin a member and the Society of Antiquaries elected Baretti. There was still a comradeship among men of letters which had persisted down the ages.

It is true that von Uffenbach declared that the great politeness which John Flamsteed, the Astronomer Royal, showed him was rare in England; but von Uffenbach thoroughly disliked everything English, and was no doubt disliked in return. He had difficulty too with the language or rather the pronunciation of it. "Owing to the difficulty of English pronunciation" he says "a stranger, however well he may understand the written language, is no better off here than if he were deaf and dumb."

Baretti tells us that for the first two months he could not understand a syllable of the language; but when he had fixed a few hundred words in his head, he made everyone he came across read out "these words, not once only but ten times and more and tried all the while to pronounce the most difficult; and thus by gradually accustoming my ears to the sound, I made what was considered extraordinary progress in that strange and most irregular tongue. . . . I have always tried to speak the dialect of every place where I have made a short stay." This was indeed an amazing feat, for dialects in those days were so distinct that the Devonian could not have understood the Yorkshireman or the Cumbrian the man from Dorset. Mrs. Thrale, however, tells a story about Baretti which bears out his assertion. " I will give " she says " an instance of his skill in our low street language. Walking in a field near Chelsea, he met a fellow, who, suspecting him from dress and manner to be a foreigner, said sneeringly ' Come sir, will you show me the way to France ? ' ' No sir' says Baretti instantly, ' but I will show you the way to Tyburn.' "

Von Uffenbach was pleasantly surprised when Sir Hans Sloane talked French to him and he comments acidly on the Englishman's disinclination to speak foreign languages, even when he knows them very well. " Ignorance and pedantry rule here " he observes with his usual sweeping bitterness.

Voltaire speaks of the unpleasant whistle of the English tongue. Moritz, though he admits that the country had many dialects and that there was even one in London, was constantly talking with people of all classes. He is often amazed at the erudition of the ordinary man. The tailor's widow who read Milton struck him with surprise; but she was nothing to the saddler, who walked with him on the road to Matlock and talked of Homer, Horace and Virgil, quoting them at length, and the poorest people, some of whom could not read, told each other stories from the Bible. They had heard the Scriptures read in Church and with the fine memory of the illiterate they could repeat them, often word for word. When men were brought up on such a Book it is no wonder that they could express themselves in " proper phrases ".

The Charity schools, established early in the century, had done a great work in teaching children at least to read and write and later the Sunday Schools, founded to impart religious knowledge, were obliged to teach their children to read the Bible. There was of course great ignorance and much illiteracy. Moritz declares that he had " conversed with several people of the lower class who all knew their national authors, and who all have read many if not all of them " ; but he also tells us how he travelled by coach with three farmers, none of whom could read or write.

Sophie de la Roche describes how she went to a Debating Society in London where sixpence a person was charged for admission and where they discussed " all topics of interest to an Englishman ". They debated as to " whether it is useful or harmful to create a number of peers of the realm as has recently happened ", and then went on to ask " whether it is better for a man to beat his wife or for a woman to control men ? " It is interesting to notice that there were women present at these debates ; what their reactions to the last question were, we are not told. Probably they took no active part in the proceedings, for it would have been thought most unseemly for a woman to speak in public.

Zetzner declared that the English were " a polite people with a developed political intelligence. They have a remarkable penetrating mind, learning and understanding everything." He adds, however, that these superior people were proud and haughty and considered themselves much above all foreigners.

Grosley, when he was in Westminster Abbey, came upon some herb women reading a little book on the monuments, and a porter passing through and looking round exclaimed, " How many lies do these stones contain ! "

On the other hand Grosley was much shocked when at Lord Byron's trial in Westminster Hall he saw boys pelting each other with apples, and even putting bits of the fruit into the Lord High Steward's enormous periwig. " I never saw " he says " youths behave in a less decent manner and appear less sensible of the dignity of a magistrate."

" I am in a new order of things ! " de Mirabeau exclaimed when he found that the Englishman had " the development and free exercise of his faculties ". It was no doubt astonishing to an aristocrat brought up in eighteenth century France, though most foreigners were surprised at the amount of learning and general cultivation displayed by the average man. They had come to England expecting to meet boors and fools and they were astonished. Their criticisms of schools and particularly of the Universities are, however, by no means so favourable.

To begin with they thoroughly disliked the architecture both at Oxford and Cambridge. It was Gothic, which they thought barbarous and was " much overloaded with ornament ". It is true that there was a young Swiss who told Sophie de la Roche that he preferred the scenery round Oxford to that of his native land; but he said nothing about the colleges.

The foreign scholar had one great and legitimate grievance. The books and parchments which he wished to consult—which indeed in some cases were the object of his visit to England—had been allowed to fall into such a shameful state of dirt and decay, that it was difficult to decipher them. All with one accord complain of this, and it illustrated, perhaps more than anything else, the low ebb to which learning had declined.

Von Uffenbach found the manuscripts at Caius lying in a garret so thick with dust that, though he had a catalogue, he could make nothing of them. He had climbed to this library up steps that were deep in pigeon's dung. The Peterhouse manuscripts were in the same disgraceful condition; but here the librarian thoughtfully provided him with a towel, which he used as an apron. The books at Magdalene were " with hardly one single exception entirely overgrown with mould ". In the Bodleian von Uffenbach found " ancient and modern coins lying all covered with dust without any order in a deep poor drawer, unlocked and left open. For all this dirt and mould he had paid eight shillings in fees. He thought it was an imposition, and was still more annoyed, for he was a poor man, at having to bribe the custodian of the Bodleian to be allowed to examine the codexes without his tiresome supervision. At Cambridge, on the other hand, he saw everything in the University Library and the attendant obligingly permitted him to take away a leaf from a damaged codex of Josephus.

" In England " Count Kielmansegg tells us " the people who show you over such places are porters and caretakers who seldom know much about them, merely show visitors round and are glad when they leave. They earn their money so easily that they show you nothing at all or only such objects as they consider worth seeing, which are usually well known things, so that the rarest objects often escape the eye and remain unobserved." This may account for the fact that von Uffenbach, when the curator of the Ashmolean had finished " toping and guzzling " and condescended to show him round, was confronted with such things as " Queen Elizabeth's shoe, King Augustus of Poland's boots, Joseph's coat, a piece of bread preserved from the siege of Oxford and a book containing the Devil's handwriting, which he identified as Chinese. Von Uffenbach thought the dining-hall at Trinity very ugly and also described it as " so smoky and smelling so strong of bread and meat that it would be impossible for me to eat a meal there ".

Magdalen (Oxford) he considers " one of the meanest here ", and the Bodleian was, in his eyes, " an old mean library ". He found the great Bentley " arrogant and disdainful ". He was not the only person who did so, many fellows of his college found the Master very arrogant. He also described the greatest classical scholar of his age as " speaking good and fairly intelligible Latin ". No doubt the English pronunciation was a stumbling block. Elie de Beaumont, the French lawyer, found the same difficulty when he went up to Oxford for his D.C.L. and tried to converse with Blackstone.

Von Uffenbach describes Cambridge as " a poor mean village ", though he admits that there were people who thought that King's College was " the finest building in the world ", and Moritz went so far as to declare that the Bodleian was not unworthy to be compared to the Vatican in Rome.

Moritz, who had been so rudely treated by landlords and pushed out of their inns, met with nothing but kindness and civility from the company assembled at the Mitre. An Oxford clergyman, whom he had met while travelling, introduced him " as a German clergyman whom he could not sufficiently praise for my correct pronounciation of the Latin, my orthodoxy and my good walking ". Moritz gave some account of the universities in his own country, admitting that riots and disturbances frequently occurred among the students. " Oh, we are very unruly here too " one of the dons remarked, taking a long drink out of his pot of beer.

Moritz, however, during his two days' stay at Oxford, thought that the conduct and behaviour of the undergraduates did them much credit. He had a less favourable impression of the dons. Their drunkenness and neglect of their duties shocked him, and that one of the company, a clergyman, should treat the Scriptures with levity disgusted him. " I have the good fortune " he says " to be able to convict him of his ignorance of its language and meaning ".

As for the learning of the Universities there are different accounts. Mme de Bocage, who took a cursory and favourable view of most things English, tells us that " whatever might interrupt the studies of the scholars, as gaming, plays and complaisant beauties, are banished from this place (Oxford). The very air of the country breathes the purest precepts of morality."

She produced this eulogy in spite of the fact that she had seen, at the Anatomical Theatre, the skeleton of a widow who had had ten husbands and was hanged for poisoning four of them.

Macky, who visited the Universities early in the century before the rot had really set in, says that " young gentlemen are obliged to all imaginable attention here (Cambridge) nay are mulcted and punished if they do not attend, whereas abroad they are left to their liberty. Another traveller compares our universities favourably with those of Germany. There even Greek Mythology and the names of Plato and Aristotle were, he declares, unknown to the average undergraduate. Learning was not quite at this low ebb in the English universities as the names of Bentley and Porson may testify, though there was a Regius Professor of Greek, who when he was appointed did not know a word of the language. He set about learning it, however, when he came up. De la Rochefoucauld has a story of a clergyman who

Drawn by F. Mackenzie *Engraved by J. Skelton*

OXFORD
MAGDALEN COLLEGE
QUEEN'S COLLEGE AND THE HIGH

came up to Cambridge for his degree of Doctor of Divinity. " He was asked " we are told " whether the sun turned round the earth, or the earth round the sun. Not knowing what to say and wanting to make some reply, he assumed an emphatic air and boldly exclaimed: ' Sometimes the one, sometimes the other.' This reply produced so much amusement that " de la Rochefoucauld declares " he was made a doctor on the strength of this fatuous stupidity." Possibly this story was untrue, but the university must have been in a very bad state before such an anecdote could be circulated. Von Uffenbach considered the state of Oxford to be very bad. " We are amazed " he says " that no courses of lectures are at all delivered and only in winter three or four lectures are given by the professors to bare walls, for no one comes in. On the other hand the scholars and students have, some of them, a professor or old socium collegis whom they call tutorem who instructs them . . . in summer however scarcely anything is done both students and professors being either in the country or in London."

Von Uffenbach asked a Cambridge professor to explain their method of teaching. He promised civilly to find out, which he never did. No doubt he cursed this inquisitive foreigner who came inquiring about method. No one worried about method at an English university, except, of course, that prating fellow Wesley, who used it in a different sense and was an Oxford man anyhow and so need not be considered. " It is a general complaint " Meister says " that the professors are indolent and without emulation and that the students in particular are negligent and under no restraint. The greater part of them are lodged in the town and lead the most dissolute lives." His democratic soul is shocked to find that the sons of noblemen have tables to themselves in the college dining halls and that these tables " are more or less elevated above the others. Kings, Cardinals and other pious founders " he says " had none of these sublime notions, which the wisdom of later ages has inculcated, and ancient customs and practices are never altered here without the greatest circumspection."

Most travellers speak of the drunkenness and debauchery which were rampant at the Universities; but Holberg the Dane, while condemning such evils, speaks of the generosity of English scholars. He tells us that when he was leaving Oxford, a fellow of Magdalen came to him and offered, on behalf of the college, any funds he might need for the continuation of his studies.

Psalmanazer had " a convenient apartment " assigned to him in one of the Oxford colleges, he does not tell us which, and was given every facility to study in the library and attend lectures. His tutor went so far as to allow him to choose the subjects of study " whether the Newtonian philosophy, logic, poetry or divinity ". Mathematics were suggested to him, but he could not be prevailed upon " to go over the threshold ", as he considered that many of Euclid's propositions were self-evident, an idea which has also occurred to several generations of schoolboys.

Of schools we do not hear a great deal, with the exception of Christ's Hospital, which foreign visitors were taken to see. Londoners were proud of this school, though the accounts of it which have come down to us from Lamb and Coleridge do not show much reason for such pride.

Sophie de la Roche comments on the excellence of the education at Christ's Hospital and this was generally admitted to be good. " A shoe-maker for instance " she exclaims " or a brewer or baker reads Virgil and Homer." As in all the great schools classics were the main subject; but Christ's Hospital had also a mathematical school for boys who were going to sea. "There" says von Uffenbach "stood a couple of fairly large ships of most elegant and curious workmanship; they can be taken to pieces, so that the children who make a special study of ship building may be shown all the parts of a ship."

Moritz visited Eton, but the only thing which seems to have impressed him there was the dress of the scholars. He describes how they all wore black cloaks or gowns over coloured clothes "through which there was an aperture for their arms. They also wore a square hat or cap that seemed to be covered with velvet such as our clergymen in many places wear." He was surprised that there were few great schools in England and at that date there were only the four public schools, Eton, Westminster, Winchester and Harrow. On the other hand there were "a prodigious number of academies. They are" he tells us, "notwithstanding their pompous names, in reality nothing more than small schools set up by private people." A master at one of these complained to Moritz that he only got £30 a year, and had nothing but water to drink. At a time when the poorest people drank beer, to be given nothing but water would have been considered the height of misery and meanness.

Many of these private schools were very bad, and the education given in them was wretched. Some, however, were well run by eighteenth-century standards, and careful parents preferred to send their children to these, rather than to the public schools, which they rightly considered to be hotbeds of vice and brutality. In any case there would not have been room in the four public schools for all the boys of upper-class parents, and there was then no idea that a gentleman's son must of necessity go to a public school.

Psalmanazer got the post of tutor to a boy of fifteen whose father, an officer in the army, " had kept him for several years at some considerable schools to little purpose, for when I came to him he could hardly translate one line out of the plainest Latin authors, which he attributed rather to the remissness of his former masters than to his want of genius ". Usually some knowledge of Latin had been flogged into a boy who went to any " considerable school ", but the English themselves were very critical of their own educational system. Adam Smith went so far as to declare that no boy at any public school ever learnt anything which would be of service to him in the world.

Of girls' education we do not hear much. Few of them went to school. The daughters of the well-to-do were generally educated at home by their mother or a governess. Some people engaged foreign teachers for their children. Grosley declares that these unfortunate ladies " who have generally refined sentiments complain very much of the indocile disposition of their scholars ". There was one large girls' school which Sophie de la Roche visited. It was in Queen's Square in London and was kept by the Misses Stevenson. " Its founders " she says " were four sisters of wealth and beauty, who said that they had no desire to marry, yet wished to become mothers according to nature's laws." What they meant by this curious statement is not explained. They had more than two hundred pupils and their fees were at least £100 a year, which was very high in those days. " The girls " Sophie tells us " are particularly fond of music and singing, adore dancing, love dress and ornament ; but are so reserved in all their other affections that it takes one a little while to get to know a girl of six or seven years of age."

One of the Misses Stevenson told Sophie that the girls

had only one holiday in the year and that she would like to abolish this, as some of them were sure to come back " with morally harmful or misguided notions ". " They tried " she added philosophically " to turn these to account as material for insight into human nature."

It was not often, unless he were residing in the country for some time, that a foreigner put his child to school in England. Casanova, however, settled his daughter at a school in Harwich. He was delighted to find that the pupils could converse with him in French and Italian; but less pleased at having to pay a hundred a year and provide the child with a bed and linen.

Moritz was delighted to find that books could be bought at cheap prices. " The quick sale of the classical authors " he says " is here promoted by cheap and convenient editions. . . . I myself bought a Milton in duo-decimo for two shillings." He also purchased two volumes of *The Vicar of Wakefield* for sixpence, and saw odd volumes of Shakespeare lying about on stalls and priced at a penny or even a halfpenny.

Von Uffenbach, however, is always complaining of the dearness of books, and of how he got his shirt ruffles filthy turning over their pages. Sophie de la Roche bought a *Handbook for Ladies* which gave directions on " How to become prosperous with Honour ". One would like to know what it recommended—probably matrimonial ventures, as these were almost the only methods by which an eighteenth-century woman could become prosperous and remain honourable.

Scholars undoubtedly came to England to study books and manuscripts. Lichtenberg went to Birmingham to see Baskerville. That great printer and binder was dead; but Lichtenberg was entertained by his widow with toast and Madeira in a finely furnished room. Dressed in a handsome black silk gown, she took him over the works and into the dirtiest corners, explaining everything except the secret which he particularly wanted to know, how the paper and ink were made. He looked, however, very carefully at the work of a woman and a little girl, who were glazing papers, and by that and a few skilful inquiries, he thought he had gathered some information. Lichtenberg would have bought the whole of the stock and machinery and transported it to Germany, if he could have afforded the £4,000 which Mrs. Baskerville was asking for it.

When Benjamin Franklin came to London early in 1724 he found that there were no circulating libraries, though these afterwards became a great feature in English life. Among the first to be founded was one in the Strand which was started in 1740 by a bookseller called Batho. Franklin, like many an Englishman who had a love of literature and little money, hung round the street bookstalls, picking up a book and reading for as long as he decently could. In the previous century Milton had described these men as " stall readers ". Many of them would wander round London from stall to stall, reading a little here, a little there, and even going so far as to turn down the page of a book or to mark it in some way so that they might return to it and read more.

The comments of foreigners on English literature are sometimes very curious. Voltaire expressed immense admiration for Wycherley's plays and compares them favourably with those of Molière, though he admits that " the rules of decorum are not so well observed ". Of Vanbrugh he says that he was " as sprightly in his writings as he was heavy in his buildings ". The language of Congreve's characters was, according to him, " that of men of honour, but their actions are those of knaves, a proof that he was perfectly acquainted with human nature and frequented what we call good society ".

He praises Pope and Swift, though he confesses that the latter can be understood by the foreigner only after a visit to England. Shakespeare was not thought much of on the Continent and the translations, including Voltaire's, of Hamlet's great speech would not have added much to the poet's fame. Voltaire really preferred Addison to Shakespeare. " Mr. Addison's *Cato* " he says " appears to me to be the greatest character that ever was brought upon any stage." At the same time he admits that " the shining monsters of Shakespeare give infinitely more delight than the judicious images of the moderns ".

Voltaire considered that learning was more honoured in England than in France. " The English " he says " have so great a veneration for exalted talents that a man of merit in their country is always sure of making his fortune." This may have been true to a certain extent; but there were many examples of Englishmen of letters and merit who eked out a miserable existence in a garret, and Mme de Bocage takes a view completely opposite to that of Voltaire. " Honours " she says " inspire people with emulation more than pensions. The English, though they are not so generous to the learned as we are, know better how to flatter their vanity. Marks of distinction encourage men of genius more than sustenance. Too much food makes them heavy; praise is a light aerial substance which strengthens and animates them. The hopes of being buried in Westminster Abbey is a powerful incentive to persons endowed with abilities to endeavour to distinguish themselves in their life time." Probably most Englishmen, whether they were geniuses or not, would have preferred a little sustenance to any tomb however distinguished.

Writing of these tombs in the Abbey, Voltaire points out that the English honoured poets and philosophers as well as Kings and conquerors.

Johnson, though he declared in his usual uncompromising manner that foreigners were fools, showed in many cases great friendship towards them. He wrote a preface to Baretti's dictionary and stood by him when he was tried for murder. He had a great respect for General Paoli, the Corsican patriot, often dining with him and going so far as to buy bigger and better shoe buckles to wear at one of his parties. The General was for many years an exile here, and was treated with much deference by the literary men of London. Eventually the government granted him a pension.

Johnson had met and drunk with George Psalmanazar, of whom we shall speak in another chapter. His opinion of Piozzi, who was a foreigner, a Roman Catholic and a singer, and who dared to marry his dear Mrs. Thrale, we know quite well. Piozzi's private thoughts on Dr. Johnson would also be interesting. When Boswell and Johnson were travelling in the post-coach with "two very agreeable ladies from America" Boswell particularly cautioned the elder not to reveal the fact that her husband had been a member of Congress " as she must know how very violent he (Johnson) was against the people of that country ". In spite of this the two ladies hung upon his words and declared that every sentence was an essay. It was only when they got to an inn and Johnson flew into a rage about the roast mutton, which was " as bad as bad could be, ill fed, ill killed, ill kept, ill dressed " that they began to wonder if he really could be a philosopher.

Of English music we do not hear much that is good. Von Uffenbach, after a visit to a music club at Cambridge, is surprised " that they make such a to-do about music and even create professors and doctors of music . . . all their compositions " he declares " are harsh and cannot equal either the pretty manner of the

French or the tender manner of the Italians and so too, this music both vocal and instrumental is very poor. The English are not much better at music than the Dutch and they are fairly bad." After hearing the organ in Trinity College Chapel, he admits that "the English excel especially herein" though he adds "whereas on all other instruments they are mean performers". Whether Miss Fours who was a pupil of Schumann came into that category we do not know. Count Kielmansegg makes no comment on that concert of hers which he attended. "She played" he tells us "entire concerts with one finger on a row of tuned wine glasses."

Von Uffenbach admits that he heard very good music at a London tavern, and saw there "two matchless clavearis worth £200 each, a hundred years old and made by Hans Rucker of Antwerp".

A London tavern may seem a strange place at which to find good music; but many of these houses had their own clubs for singing and instrumental music or they would hire really good performers.

It must be admitted that the English did not think much of their own music. That the great Handel should have been welcomed and acclaimed was only his just due; but many mediocre performers were run after simply because they were foreign. Addison expressed strong disapproval of the Italian singers at the opera; but all London flocked to hear them. Lichtenberg speaks of "that tinsel nutshell of a world, the Italian opera", where he saw Dido Gabrieli, the Roman prima donna, "in gold and white silk, who rushed along at the head of a silver clad Carthaginian guard amid the applause of all London".

Foreign singers and musicians could command large salaries. Vanneschi, the Italian manager of Covent Garden, received three hundred guineas for the book of one of the operas. True he had to give a portion to his countryman Rolli; but the usual price, Walpole tells us, was fifty guineas. He was also allowed another three hundred guineas to go to Italy to pick up a cast. He returned with dancers and singers and also with a tailor as he declared that there were none in London. In spite of this slur on our sartorial talents the tailor was actually received and given four hundred pounds. Another Italian named Buggiani with his daughter and a fellow countryman returned to Italy after being in this country for three or four years. We are told that they " had made enough money to load a mule ". Giannetta Bacchelli, the Italian dancer, had such a fascination for the Duke of Dorset that he brought her to England with him, installed her at Knole, and to the horror of his family, gave her his Garter to wear as a hair ribbon with " *honi soit qui mal y pense* " in diamonds.

One of the results of the popularity of the Italian opera was that the Italian language was more widely studied. Educated men had learnt Italian; but now women began to study it too and often took candles with them to the opera in order to be able to follow the book. It strikes us as a dangerous practice and many dresses must have been ruined by candle-grease.

On the other hand Mme de Bocage tells us that " English words were sung by Italian performers ". She declared that the Italian opera gave her much less pleasure than oratorios and that " the declamation of the recitative makes us buy dearly a few pleasing airs, with which it terminates ". She describes the entrance of Handel at one of his oratorios and how wax candles were carried before him and placed upon his organ. " Amidst a loud clapping of hands " she says " he seats himself, and the whole band of music strikes up at exactly the same moment. At the interlude he plays concertos of his own composition, either alone or accompanied by the orchestra. These are equally admirable for the harmony and the execution."

Handel's rival, Buononcini, was thought by some to surpass the great master himself; but his popularity did not last. He left England under a cloud, having been accused of plagiarism.

Johann Christian Bach came to London in 1762 and gave a series of concerts and some of his own operas which were thought very fine. Many music lovers, who had scarcely heard of his father the great Bach, flocked to his concerts, talked about his exposition of the Manheim school, his fifteen operas and the oratorio he had written. He became music master to the Royal family and had many other pupils.

Baretti complains of the harshness of the English voice and the Englishman's ignorance of music. " Their Beard, Campness, Miss Young and Mrs. Cibber " he says " would frighten you out of your senses if you heard them sing on the stage. Would you believe it that among all the thousands of beautiful women and young girls who gather here (London) from every part of the island in winter hardly a dozen have good voices, yet they have a passion for singing and hearing music, and pay highly for it and they fight against nature itself in making it the chief element in a woman's education. Most absurd of all, their faces remain as impassive as marble when they hear the best Italian singers."

An English audience would, no doubt, have appeared cold and undemonstrative to an Italian; but that the English cared for music there can be no doubt; the existence of the many music clubs and the large attendance at concerts is proof of this. Music, as Baretti says, was part of the education of all girls in the upper and middle classes. It enhanced their value as wives if they were able to play and sing to their husbands and their guests after dinner. No doubt a great many girls had music forced upon them when they had no taste or even ear for it; but that was the case in all other educational subjects. Boys were forced to learn the classics who had no aptitude for them, and they would have found it difficult to get even a smattering of science however much they might have desired it.

If the foreign traveller tells us little about English music, he tells us even less about English art. Probably he considered it beneath his notice, for English painters were hardly known on the Continent. Baretti indeed admired Sir Joshua Reynolds. He speaks of Thrale's collection of portraits at Streatham as " all presented in the highest style of this great master ".

In 1769 Baretti was appointed by the King (George III) Secretary for foreign correspondence to the Royal Academy, which had just been founded. This post carried no salary; but it was considered an honour and Baretti's appointment, which seems to have been popular, shows that, among artists at least, there was no prejudice against foreigners.

As in music so in art, native productions were held in low esteem even by Englishmen. Collectors preferred foreign paintings and when a man made a Grand Tour or visited the Continent later in life he generally brought back French or Italian works of art. He even preferred copies of Raphael or Andrea del Sarto to pictures by native artists. True, he might have his portrait or those of his family painted by Gainsborough or Romney, and Sir Joshua Reynolds was a fashionable painter, who would charge as much as two hundred guineas for a full length; but the wealthy Englishman looked upon English portraits as we regard photographs, and with the exception of Reynolds, did not think much of the men who painted them.

When the foreigner mentions art in England, he is generally admiring pictures which have been brought from the Continent. " A great part " says Meister " of the most admired labours of Greece and Italy and of Rome, both ancient and modern, have for a century past been transported to this new Carthage, and are actually to be met with in the villas of this happy island." The foreign decorative painters Ricci, Angelica Kauffman and Zucci set the fashion in England for frescoes and painted ceilings and the best of this work was executed by foreigners.

Many travellers criticized our architecture, as we have seen, and for the most part thought poorly of it. This is surprising when we consider how often the rich Englishman had provided copies of Italian architecture for their admiration.

" The heroes " Mme de Bocage says " in whose honour the city of London creates statues shine only by their reputation and not by the ability of the sculptors ", and she considers " that correctness and elegance in writing and a just taste in architecture, painting and sculpture are still in their infant state ".

CHAPTER 8

The Poor, Hospitals, Charities

THE poorer classes are described by many foreigners as well fed and well dressed, even at the end of the century when destitution was widespread. Probably the traveller never penetrated into the slums and saw the state of filth and misery in which the very poor lived. Still, as we may see from Hogarth's plates, the destitute were to be found everywhere. They jostled the gentleman in his velvet and laces as he walked the streets, they rubbed shoulders with him at prize-fights and bull-baitings, crowds of beggars swarmed in every city. We must conclude that the condition of the poor was not so bad in England as in some continental countries.

" There were very few poor in London " Grosley tells us, and Moritz says that the neat villages and small towns suggested opulence.

" The feet of the peasants " Voltaire notes " are not bruised by wooden shoes, they eat white bread, are well clothed and are not afraid of increasing their stock of cattle nor of tiling their houses from any apprehension that their taxes will be raised the year following."

Meister even quotes a certain Count D—— who complained on returning to his native land that their most celebrated criminals did not go to the gallows so well dressed as the commonest English thief. " I rarely see " Moritz says " even a fellow with a wheelbarrow who has not a shirt on." The poor man in England, Meister tells us, was better clothed, lodged and fed than his contemporary in France. As he had more food he worked better and there were fewer holidays in England than in France. This was true as regards holidays, especially towards the end of the century. In Catholic countries there were still many church festivals when no work was done. In England, since the Reformation, such holidays had dwindled in number, until at the end of the eighteenth century they were very few indeed. The country labourer might take a day or two off at Christmas, and make holiday on May Day and at the parish feast; but in London and the larger towns Good Friday was often the only day besides Sunday which a workman could call his own.

Even the beggars, according to de Saussure, were well off. He speaks of one who had amassed a thousand pounds, a very large sum in those days. Perhaps he was a myth, at any rate he must have been an exception, for when de Saussure visited England about the middle of the century there were many beggars, and it is obvious that they could not all have made fortunes. Baretti, who was more observant, gives a different account. " In spite " he says " of the hospitals and the vast amount spent in private charity and the heavy sums paid by the poor law, there are enough of them (indigent people) to fill a province. This is not an exaggeration."

He always carried a pocket full of small change to give to beggars though he could often ill afford it. Baretti was fortunate enough to make the acquaintance of the great Fielding, when he was magistrate at Bow Street, and he inquired of him whether some of the beggars whom he saw in the streets did not die of hunger. " Over a thousand or even two thousand of them in a year " Fielding answered, " but London is so large it is barely noticed." It is curious that Baretti was almost the only foreigner to realize the miserable condition of the London poor. Were they so much worse off than the poor of his native Piedmont? Had Piedmont, had Venice, which he knew so well, no beggars, no starving poor? It is difficult to believe this. Probably with their small populations, their lovely surroundings and their sunshine the Italian cities looked more prosperous. At any rate they had no fog and black rain, no inky mud to emphasize their misery.

Grosley complains of the rudeness of the mob, particularly towards foreigners, and of such expressions as French dog and French b—— which were hurled at them. A Portuguese, taking a walk by the riverside and speaking his native language, was confronted by two watermen who doubled their fists at him: " French dog " they exclaimed, " speak your damned French if you dare!" Grosley contrasts this outrageous behaviour with the politeness of the upper classes and the civility of shopkeepers and he admits that the English poor could be very rude and violent towards their own countrymen. He describes how a mob in Seven Dials, disappointed because a man had not been put in the pillory, threw the dead dogs and rotten eggs, which they had been saving up for him, at the passing coaches and foot passengers.

In spite of this episode Grosley praises the comparative order of the London streets, though there were no troops, guards or patrols to keep order. He even goes so far as to declare that " London is the only great city in Europe where neither murder nor assassination happen ". It is plain that Grosley could not have read the newspapers; but as regards the safety of the London streets he is borne out by Meister, who says that "a constable armed only with a single staff of his authority effects more here in London than all the crimson ensigns of our august municipality are able to do in Paris. He met " he says " with fewer disturbances and affrays in a fortnight in London than in one morning in Paris."

The animus against the French, which was exemplified in the rudeness and intolerance of the mob, can be easily understood. France had for so long been the enemy; she was a Catholic country, she might invade England and set up bonfires in Smithfield, or, what was almost as bad and more probable, settle among the English and undercut them. There was the example of the Huguenots before their eyes, though they, of course, were Protestants and had to be tolerated. With the French were naturally confounded all foreigners, though exceptions were often made. Benjamin Franklin was much respected by his fellow workmen, though he was an American and only drank water. The negro slaves who came to England and who, after Lord Mansfield's famous judgment, remained here as free men, did not complain of any colour bar. The English lower classes regarded them with kindliness and tolerance and sometimes intermarried with them.

If the foreigner was often critical of our customs and way of life, he usually had nothing but praise for our charities and the methods by which the poor were provided for in England. Macky, after mentioning " A noble Hospital for Decayed Habidashers ", goes on to tell us that there were " more almshouses in and about London than in all the cities of Holland which prided itself on them ".

" No rich person " de Saussure says " dies without leaving large legacies. Most parishes in London and the country have hospitals for the sick, the poor and the aged, also charity schools, where poor children are fed, taught and clothed." When de Saussure speaks of country hospitals he is probably referring to some kind of almshouse, for at the date when he writes, the middle of the century, there were very few hospitals anywhere out of London. There was the Bath Hospital, which was, Count Kielmansegg tells us, " for poor indigent patients of all kinds who have to take the waters. . . . The inmates are well cared for free of charge and enjoy every comfort." As the century advanced more hospitals were built both in London and in the country towns.

Sophie de la Roche tells us of a Maternity Hospital for the wives of the London poor which certainly exceeded in generosity and the length of care bestowed anything of the kind in our own day. The women were taken in a fortnight before their confinements were expected, " being nourished meanwhile with strengthening foods, so as to live through their child-bed, and for six whole weeks they are given a good bed with nice, white linen and all possible attention. They are finally presented with a cot and swaddling clothes for the child."

These lying-in hospitals were generally well managed. From them came the maternity nurses who attended the well-to-do, and a ladies' committee superintended their organization.

The Foundling Hospital was one of the sights to which foreigners were taken. This hospital, built in Lamb's Conduit Fields, so that its inmates might enjoy pure country air, was one of the beautiful things of London and it lasted until the philistine authorities of our own day suffered it to be destroyed. As early as 1713 Addison, in an essay in the *Guardian*, had called attention to the plight of unwanted infants, who were often exposed to die upon the highway. It was not, however, till 1742 that, thanks to the exertions of Captain Thomas Coram, a place of refuge to be called the Foundling Hospital was

THE QUEEN'S HOUSE, ST. JAMES'S PARK
THE FOUNDLING HOSPITAL

built by public subscriptions. Three of Hogarth's pictures, which that great painter had presented to the Hospital, hung upon its walls; Handel had given an organ for the chapel and every year a benefit of his oratorio, *The Messiah*, which he conducted himself.

Sophie de la Roche describes it with her usual enthusiasm. She says that "the children looked bright and attractive and very healthy; that the beds were clean, the air pure" and everything looked so nice. The elder girls had laid the tables in very pretty, spacious dining rooms, everything was white and spotless; other girls did the waiting; the meal only consisted of one course of mutton boiled with barley; but it was so well prepared and in such quantities that with their good bread and mug of beer the children could not want for anything better."

The Foundling was, by eighteenth-century standards, very well managed, and was far better than the workhouses which were the only other refuge for abandoned children, and where they so often perished miserably. Needless to say, these institutions were not shown to foreigners.

Greenwich Hospital excited general admiration for the beauty of its architecture and internal decoration. It was opened in 1705 for the reception of fifty-two sailors of the Royal Navy and the Mercantile Marine who had been wounded in battle. "Nothing is wanting" Meister says "that can lend to the production of repose and conservation of health" and Count Kielmansegg goes into greater detail concerning the internal arrangements. "There are" he says "partitions contrived like small wooden ship's cabins, sufficient to contain a bed, a table and a chest of clothes, so that all the men sleep separately, though during the day they are together. Very few sailors, I believe, have been so well housed before, for every man is allowed per week 7 lb. of bread 3 lb. of beef 2 lb. of mutton and a pint of peas 1¾ lb. of cheese 2 oz. of butter 14 quarts of beer and a shilling for tobacco. Those who have been boatswains mates or other petty officers are allowed in proportion 1*s.* 6*d.* and 2*s.* 6*d.* for tobacco. They receive also every other year, a blue suit, a hat, three pairs of socks, two pairs of shoes, five neckties, three shirts and two nightcaps." The authorities seem to have been mean about butter, but the allowance of meat was more than ample ; indeed in these restricted days it seems surprising that a man could eat 5 lb. of meat in a week, even allowing for large proportions of bone and gristle.

Bedlam, incredible as it may seem, was one of the sights of London. The gentle, kindly Sophie de la Roche paints it in softened if not glowing colours. There were, she said, no chains or straps, though the worst of the patients wore strait-jackets, which were tied with cords to the corners of the rooms. These rooms were bright and comfortable and the inmates were encouraged to read and occupy themselves quietly. Sophie found Mrs. Nicholson, who had tried to murder George III, reading Shakespeare, and asking for some more quill pens. The man at that time in charge of the asylum was Dr. Monroe, who insisted on fresh air and cleanliness, and that the patients should be treated kindly. " This " he told Sophie " is a fever of the mind, tender, gentle handling is the only cure for this." Unfortunately very few doctors agreed with Monroe and when he was not at Bedlam things were very different. De Saussure saw dangerous maniacs chained and terrible to behold. " On holidays " he says " numerous persons of both sexes, but belonging generally to the lower classes, visit the hospital and amuse themselves by watching these unfortunate wretches who often give them cause for laughter." Von Uffenbach says that "in Holland such places are managed with far greater propriety".

The open-handed charity of the English struck many foreigners. "Their humanity has been clearly proved during the present war" Baretti says; "a voluntary subscription was made by the whole nation to clothe the many thousands of their enemies who were kept prisoners in this island, and who, without these liberal contributions from all classes, would for the most part, have died of cold last winter, which was very severe. What nation, ancient or modern, has ever given the world such an example of heroic charity? ... The truth is that the English do their utmost to make money; but once they have made it, they spend it freely, and will give it to you if you ask them for it ... when they are convinced that you are an honest man; whether you are a foreigner or one of themselves, they make a point of supporting you and advancing you."

CHAPTER 9

English Towns

MANY foreigners stopped short at London and saw no more of England. Others, as we have seen, visited the Universities. There were a few who made an extended tour of the country, visiting such places as Bath, Tunbridge Wells, the cathedral cities and other towns. Some came on business and journeyed to the manufacturing centres. These travellers came, for the most part, in the latter half of the century. In early days manufactures were mainly the products of the country. Villages made not only their own bread and beer, their saddlery, carts, furniture and leather goods; but wove cloth, linen and cotton fabrics, which were sent to the towns for distribution.

Bristol disposed of the cloth goods which came from the Cotswold country. Leeds and Halifax collected bales of stuff from the Yorkshire dales, and factors assured Macky that they got £30,000 from London every week for materials made near Colchester. Exeter specialized in serges and gloves. Baretti was told that serges of the value of £100,000 had been sold there in a week, and that they were exported to Catholic countries to make habits for monks and nuns. He also declared that he saw several store-houses in that city "which contained as many bales of serge as would have sufficed to make an entrenchment round the camp of the Austrians".

INDUSTRIAL TOWNS

There were, of course, even in the early days of the century, some towns and cities which were, at least partially, industrial. London had its china and pottery works at Chelsea, Bow and Lambeth, Birmingham was a manufacturing city. Before the industrial revolution, there were children of seven or eight being employed in candlemaking at Frome in Somerset. We are told that they earned half a crown a week, and that four hundred were employed.

Travellers, who came from less industrialized countries, were shocked at the conditions prevailing in English manufacturing towns. Faujas de St. Fond says that the dirt, fog, noise and miserable condition of the workers frightened and distressed foreign visitors. This was in 1784, when the industrial revolution, growing steadily if sporadically, had cast its dark shadow over " England's green and pleasant land " and over the lives of thousands of the inhabitants.

Visitors from the Continent who wished to examine our industries were frequently disappointed. Faujas de St. Fond, who, in spite of their horrible surroundings, was anxious to see the cotton mills at Soho, near Birmingham, was refused admission and when he protested he was told that a French colonel, when taken round the works, had been detected making drawings surreptitiously of some of the machinery. Frederick the Great, who wanted to introduce steam power in his mines, sent men to steal or bribe their way into the secrets of Watt's engine. Baron von Stein had tried to get particulars of the plant used at Barclay and Perkins's brewery and had also endeavoured to entice away one of the workmen from Bolton's works.

The extraordinary advance of English manufactures had not been unnoticed on the Continent, and it was the wonder and envy of other nations. They wanted to know the secret of it, and there were few, if any, who could have told them. Most Englishmen would have suggested, and sometimes quite politely, that it was due to the innate genius of the English people, others would have murmured something about the near proximity of iron and coal in the north of England, though they would have been reminded that there was a lot of iron and coal to be found and often near together both in France and Prussia. Perhaps there was something in the English character which predisposed men like Watts and Cartwright, Trevethick and Jethro Tull to invent and introduce mechanical appliances which were to revolutionize English manufactures and the practice of agriculture. The influence of the Royal Society, too, did much to encourage scientific inquiry and invention. Founded in the reign of Charles II and under the patronage of the King and his uncle Prince Rupert, it was in the van of discovery, though some men were heard to murmur that the members had divergent views, and spoke with an uncertain voice.

Although some works were barred to them the interested foreigner was able to visit several mills and factories. Von Uffenbach went to see pins made. " To begin with " he says " we saw the English pins, which are so much liked by all females ", and he gives a long description of how they were made, of course by hand. English pins were much appreciated by foreigners, who seemed to find difficulty in making them. They were expensive, but a necessity for every woman in an age when clothes were pinned across the person, and buttons and other fastenings not much used.

Von Uffenbach also saw taffeta, damask and velvet being made, and mentions the small children who worked so wonderfully.

Lichtenberg, more fortunate than Faujas de St. Fond,

was admitted into Bolton's works at Birmingham. He saw the new steam engine which raised 20,000 cubic feet of water to a great height. He also watched the manufacture of buttons, watch-chains, sword hilts and watches as well as papier-maché snuff-boxes, tea caddys and the bodies of coaches. He was one of the travellers who complained of the horrible noise of the factories and of the bad conditions in which the people worked. Sophie de la Roche did not speak of any bad conditions when she visited Wedgwood's factory, indeed she broke into one of her not infrequent pæans, and declared " that the Briton is born for all that is noble is a true and not a biased statement ".

She might well be moved by the beauty of Wedgwood ware, and in the days of the great Josiah, and under his rule and that of his successors factory conditions were some of the best.

Faujas de St. Fond met Watt and Priestley at Birmingham. He also speaks of the Huguenots who, he tells us, " were allured into England and Germany by toleration, liberty of worship and sound policy ".

They certainly added much to the wealth and prosperity of manufacturing England. Other things besides pins were appreciated on the Continent, notably cloth and serges. Campe speaks of a suit of clothes and a hat which he had inherited. " A blue suit " he says " which my father brought from London at the beginning of the last (the eighteenth) century fell to me and my brothers in the years 1750 to 1760 for Sunday use, after having been worn by my father for forty years. As one boy grew out of them they descended to the next. I was the third in succession. Both, when they came to me were so little worn that for some years they still made me swell with pride and attracted envious looks. The cloth appeared to be made of the softest leather, and where the surface had rubbed new hair always appeared since the whole hat was made throughout of hair down to the last fibre."

The status of the merchant and shopkeeper surprised foreigners. On the Continent there was generally a wide gulf between the upper classes and those engaged in trade. In England, in the early part of the century, this was not the case. The younger sons of country gentlemen often became merchants and shopkeepers. There were few openings in the army or the professions and the idea that there was anything derogatory in trade came in with the Hanoverians and only slowly permeated English society. "When Lord Townshend was minister of state" Voltaire tells us "a brother of his was content to be a city merchant. This custom, which begins however to be laid aside, appears monstrous to Germans, vainly puffed up with their extraction." De Saussure was astonished to find gentlemen and the younger sons of peers engaged in commerce. "Some merchants" he says "are certainly far wealthier than many sovereign princes of Germany and Italy."

The English merchant, though he might be wealthy and live in great comfort, was seldom ostentatious. This would have been considered unbecoming and might have raised doubts as to his solvency. He dressed soberly, usually worked very hard, and in the early days of the century lived in the city over his place of business.

"No walls, no gates, no sentries, no garrisons" is Pastor Moritz's delighted comment on the cities of England.

Some travellers might have no concern with manufacturers, but have wished to see something of English country towns. They showed little interest in architecture; Meister described Salisbury Cathedral as a "glaring building" though he admired its spire. Stratford-on-Avon had become a place of pilgrimage and some foreign travellers went to see it. Lichtenberg tells us how he sat on Shakespeare's chair from which people were beginning to cut away pieces. He made the custodian cut some fragments for him, for which he paid a shilling. He would, he said, have them made into rings. When Pastor Moritz visited Stratford he found that the chair had been so much cut about that it no longer resembled a chair. This, however, did not deter him from taking away a small piece which, one is glad to know, he afterwards lost. The souvenir hunter was an even greater menace in those days then he is in these.

If foreigners went for a tour of pleasure they usually included in it some spa or watering-place. The most popular resort was Bath. The elder Wood had begun to rebuild this beautiful city in 1724, and a few years later it was attracting a concourse of people including some foreigners. In 1750 the stage-coach would convey passengers from London to Bath in three days, and by 1776, the time had been reduced to twenty hours.

"The Bath people" Macky tells us "live entirely on strangers" and certainly everything was done for their comfort and entertainment. Any distinguished visitor arriving at Bath was greeted by a peal of bells from the Abbey, and early on the following morning, he was serenaded by a band outside his lodgings. Both the bellringers and the musicians expected a handsome remuneration. Thanks to the architectural developments of the two Woods, their patron Ralph Allen and the exertions of that King of Bath, Beau Nash, the old dilapidated houses had been swept away, the paths cleaned and repaired and a horde of beggars and footpads swept from the streets. So safe was it that ladies could even venture to walk about the city unattended and Beau

Nash insisted that all gentlemen should lay aside their swords when at Bath. He also drew up a list of rules, which everyone in the town was expected to observe. It says much for his strength of purpose and for the awe which he inspired that so many of these rules were actually obeyed. The eighteenth century did not like to be dragooned and had little respect for laws to say nothing of mere rules. It is true that they were very cleverly drawn up ; Nash's first rule was " That a visit of ceremony at first coming and another at going away are all that is expected of ladies of quality and fashion except impertinents ".

" 2. That ladies coming to the ball appoint a time for their footman coming to wait on them home to prevent disturbance and inconveniences to themselves and others.

" 3. That gentlemen of fashion never appearing in gowns and caps show breeding and respect.

" 4. That no person takes it ill that anyone goes to another's play or breakfast and not theirs, except captious by nature.

" 5. That no gentleman gives his ticket for the balls to any but a gentlewoman. N.B. unless he has none of his acquaintance.

" 6. That gentlemen crowding before the ladies at the balls show ill manners and that none do so for the future except such as respect no one but themselves.

" 7. That no gentleman or lady takes it ill that another dances before them, except such as have no pretence to dance at all.

" 8. That the elder ladies and children be content with the second bench at the ball, as being past or not come to perfection.

" 9. That the younger ladies take notice how many eyes observe them. N.B. this does not apply to the ' Have at alls '.

BATH IN THE EIGHTEENTH CENTURY

" 10. That all whisperers of lies and scandals be taken for their authors.

" 11. That all repeaters of such lies and scandals be shunned by all company except such as have been guilty of the same crimes. N.B. several men of no character, old women and young ones of questioned reputation are great authors of lies in these places, being of the sect of the levellers."

Macky gives us an interesting picture of the life at Bath. " In the morning early " he says " the company of both sexes meet at the Pump Room, in a great hall inrailed and drink the waters and saunter about till prayer time, or divert themselves by looking at those that are bathing in the bath. Most of the company go to church in the morning in dishabille and then go home to dress for walks before dinner. The walks are behind the church, spacious and well shaded, planted round with shops, filled with everything that contributes to pleasure and at the end a noble room for gaming, from whence there are hanging stairs to a pretty garden for everyone, the time they stay, to walk in." Macky wonders why physicians prescribe gaming for their patients, and supposes that it is to keep their minds free from business cares and the ordinary worries of life, though he would have thought that " one cross throw at play must sour a man's blood more than ten glasses of water well sweetened ". " The King and Queen's Baths " he continues " are the baths where people of common rank go in promiscuously, and indeed everybody except the first quality. The way of going into them is very comical. A chair with a couple of chairmen come to your bedside be in what storey you will, and there strip you and give you their dress without your shift, and wrapping you in blankets carry you to the bath." " The steam of the bath, which ascended in clouds, the slime and stench, the multitude of people with only their heads and hands above the water" reminded Macky of pictures of purgatory. From a hygienic point of view the effects of crowding masses of people, many of whom were far from clean, in the one bath must have been extremely bad. The authorities did, however, draw the line somewhere and had a separate bath, Macky tells us, for lepers. Leprosy was becoming rare in England and the bath was a relic from earlier days. Had not Bladud, a British prince, been cured of leprosy by the hot springs of Bath? Diagnosis in the eighteenth century was elementary and we may suppose that anyone with a repulsive skin disease whose presence might have raised a riot in the common bath was consigned to the lepers. There was a hospital at Bath for " poor indigent persons " Kielmansegg tells us ; " the inmates are well cared for free of charge and enjoy every comfort ". " Many women came to Bath " Macky says " hoping that the treatment might give them children. Others came from curiosity or for less innocent reasons " and he mentions a Lady —— who told Dr. Radcliffe when he asked what she went to Bath for " only for wantonness, doctor ". " And pray Madam did it cure you " he inquired. Dr. Radcliffe was noted for his outspokenness. He it was who had told the Princess Anne that her illness was nothing but the vapours. Other doctors were more accommodating and were quite ready to recommend Bath to their patients. The Abbé le Blanc tells a correspondent " that a visit to Bath is very probably the result of six months of intrigue and consideration. The fair patient has had to feign illness, to win over servants, to corrupt a doctor, to persuade an aunt, to deceive a husband . . . she naturally seeks compensation for all the trouble she has taken. " Ladies " he assured his friend " are different beings at Bath, no longer melancholy."

Bristol was but a short journey from Bath, and some visitors may have gone there to see the city or drink from the hot springs. These became fashionable in the reign of Anne who granted the city a charter in 1710. Cheltenham was visited by George III in 1788, and this made its fortune as a spa though its great days were in the following century.

Tunbridge Wells was a lesser Bath. In the previous century Queen Henrietta Maria had retired there to drink the waters after the birth of Prince Charles. She had made it fashionable and fashionable it continued to be. The journey from London was comparatively short and easy, the little town was pleasantly situated among wooded hills and the chalybeate springs were considered to be most beneficial to many ailments. Beau Nash visited the Wells and tried to make it a second Bath. He introduced many of the social practices which he had established in the " Queen city ", including daily services in church.

The season in Tunbridge Wells lasted from the end of May till the end of September. As at most of the health resorts those taking the waters got up early in the morning. Fashionable ladies, who seldom, in the ordinary way, rose till noon found themselves gazing out of their bedroom windows at the rising sun. They then went out on to the Pantiles and drank the waters, they took a turn on the walks, which, according to Macky, were " crowded with gay and glittering company ". Most of them attended Divine Service and it was not until after this round of water drinking, parading and church-going that the fashionable company sat down to breakfast. During the remainder of the morning there was more strolling on the Pantiles with visits to mercers and milliners or to the booksellers. One of the latter kept a book in which the young men, who frequented the place, wrote verses to various ladies or in praise of the fair sex in general. This was open to inspection and it was the ambition of many a girl to see her name and charms thus celebrated. After dinner the company paraded again up and down the Pantiles dressed as if for a party. There were balls twice a week at the Assembly Rooms, and card parties and assemblies on the other nights, Sundays of course excepted.

Writing from Tunbridge Wells Elizabeth Montagu says: "Here are Hungarians, French, Portuguese, Irish and Scotch . . . I never saw a worse collection of human creatures in my life." The same pleasant informality reigned at Tunbridge Wells as at Bath. Macky tells us that " you engage with the ladies at play without any introduction only they do not admit of visits at their lodgings, but every gentleman is received by the fair sex upon the walks ".

At Epsom, he tells us, such visits were received. Epsom had, however, already begun to deteriorate. In the seventeenth century it was a quiet spa where a few people came to drink the waters and enjoy the air. In 1706 a certain John Livingston, an apothecary, conceived the idea of making it a fashionable resort. He sank a new well, erected Assembly Rooms and other buildings where dicing and all kinds of card games could be indulged in. With these diversions, balls and routs, good shops and good music, Livingston hoped to attract the nobility and gentry. For a time he succeeded; but it began to be said that the waters of this new well that he had opened were not nearly so efficacious as those of the old one. Horse racing was permanently established at Epsom in 1730, though meetings had been held there occasionally since the reign of James I. An eighteenth-century racecourse was infested by every kind of rough and sharper and the ladies who received promiscuous visits in their rooms would have been of the class which frequented these places. Macky declared that the " town of Epsom was swarming with that vermin called Sharpers ". The nobility and gentry, who had never come in large numbers, fled away.

Hampstead had the same unenviable reputation. From being a country village, largely inhabited by laundresses, it became a spa. The waters, which contained iron, magnesia and lime, were thought to be " beneficial for diseases arising from languor of the circulation or general debility of the system ". There were concerts and dances in the Long Rooms, races on the Heath and entertainments at Belsize; but its nearness to the metropolis, even though the road was bad and dangerous, attracted an undesirable crowd. " Its nearness to London " Macky complained " brings so many loose women in vamped up old clothes to catch the city apprentice that modest company are ashamed to appear there." This is probably an exaggeration. There was good company to be found at the Wells and the Assembly Rooms. The Kit-Kat Club met at the Upper Flask Inn and a small but distinguished society was to be found at Hampstead. Chatham lived at North End. Butler of the Analogy, Joanna Baillie, Steel, Constable and Romney all lived in the neighbourhood. Von Uffenbach, who is not usually a flattering critic, gives a more favourable picture of Hampstead or Hempstede as he calls it. " It is such an agreeable spot " he says " that not only do many people take the waters there, but several have built handsome houses for themselves. . . . Everything goes very well, and altho' many harlots ply their trade there . . . the other females are not ashamed to dance in the same rooms with them. Nothing is danced but the new English contre-dances or, as they should really be called country dances, and they are, for the most part, very charming."

Hampstead certainly deteriorated as the century advanced. The road from London was so much infested by highwaymen and footpads that respectable people and those who had anything to lose often hesitated to brave its dangers. Towards the end of the century, when the highways improved and journeys did not take so long, the upper classes preferred Bath or Tunbridge Wells and fashion forsook Hampstead. The same change applied to Richmond. Pieter Burmann tells us that there was a great crowd at the mineral springs, there was dancing every Monday and Thursday night; but he does not describe the company. Probably they were small city shopkeepers, apprentices, and a large number of the usual pimps, prostitutes and pick-pockets who frequented the less reputable spas.

In the north Buxton and Harrogate were two of the chief health resorts. Faujas de St. Fond went to Buxton and he did not like it at all. "It is situated" he tells us "in the midst of the most dismal and cheerless country that I know. Its waters may be excellent; but most certainly the air one breathes is impregnated with sorrow and misery. The houses, almost all uniform, look like hospitals or rather monkish buildings." De St. Fond eflects the usual opinions of his age; wild landscape, moors and crags were considered barbarous and dismal. The early Gothic revival did nothing for them. It stimulated admiration for soft undulating pastures, woods, streams and real or artificial ruins; but it needed the pen of Walter Scott to attract his readers to the wild country north of the border or later to the moors of Derbyshire and Yorkshire.

Early in the century a few doctors began to recommend sea bathing and even the drinking of sea water as beneficial to health. The practice spread until it became a fashion and in 1750 Beale set up his bathing machines at Margate. These wooden cabins on wheels were drawn into the sea by horses, a large hood protruded over the water and in this circumscribed space women bathers clad in heavy serge gowns from neck to feet could splash about. Men sometimes used these contrivances especially if they could not swim, and in the eighteenth century the majority could not. Those men who could swam out into the sea, in a state of nature which made it impossible for women to venture beyond their hoods. Macky went to Great Yarmouth, but whether for the purpose of bathing he does not say. He describes the " Yarmouth coaches " as they were called. These were long narrow vehicles, gaily painted and specially constructed to pass through the narrow rows or small streets of the town. " What they call their coach here " he says ". is very comical. It is a wheel-barrow drawn by one horse without any covering in which they carry you all over the town and to the seaside for sixpence." These coaches were killed by the tax on pleasure vehicles imposed at the close of the century.

Sea bathing was given another advertisement in 1753 when Dr. Russell published his book on *Glandular consumption and the Use of Sea Water in Diseases of the Glands*. The effect of this and other medical treatises on the subject was the founding of the Sea Bathing Hospital at Margate. Whether foreigners availed themselves of this cure we do not know, but it is improbable. Medical men on the Continent and for that matter in England were usually of the opinion that consumption was incurable, or if the patient's condition could be improved it would only be by keeping him in a very warm room from which fresh air was carefully excluded. Dr. Russell was an innovator and his ideas about the efficacy of sea water and fresh air were never popular.

CHAPTER 10

The Foreigner in the Country

LONDON was the chief and to some travellers perhaps the only attraction, but there were others who journeyed through the country on pleasure or business, and a few who were interested in agriculture. Some stayed in country houses; De la Rochefoucauld did so, and had a poor opinion of them. " All the castles " he says, and by castles he doubtless means the seats of the nobility and gentry, " that I have seen in England are great masses of brick, with innumerable windows let into them. From outside they are extremely gloomy and mostly very old. There is no evidence of growth or of the handiwork of a skilful architect; they are impressive but nothing more."

" The cleanliness which pervaded everything was a perpetual source of satisfaction ", until on one unlucky day de la Rochefoucauld penetrated into the kitchen of a country house. " The dirt " he declares " is indescribable. Women are usually employed and are as black as coal, their arms bared to the elbow are disgustingly dirty; to save time they handle the portions of food with their hands."

One feels that he must have been unfortunate in the kitchen which he selected, eighteenth-century ladies were usually most particular about the condition of their kitchens, and looked after dirt very carefully. If they were of too exalted a station to superintend everything themselves they employed housekeepers, and it would have been a very careless and incompetent woman who would have allowed the cooking to be carried on under such disgusting conditions.

De la Rochefoucauld describes the day as he spent it in country houses. It was the same routine, he said, whether he was staying with the Duke of Grafton at Euston or with a plain country gentleman. Breakfast was at nine o'clock and even the ladies came down to it, fully dressed and with their hair properly done. Breakfast consisted merely of tea and bread and butter, with possibly chocolate or coffee in really opulent establishments. The morning newspapers were on the table, de la Rochefoucauld tells us, " and those who want to do so, read them during breakfast, so that conversation is not of a lively nature ". Hunting, shooting, fishing and walking occupied the day.

" One of the Englishman's greatest joys " de la Rochefoucauld tells us " is in field sports . . . they are all quite mad about them." He hunted with the Duke of Grafton's pack and he tells us that the Duke had " forty couples of magnificent hounds ", which cost about ten or twelve guineas a pair. He says that hunting people thought nothing of riding fifty or sixty miles, and that often at the end of the day their horses were too much exhausted to bring them home, and they were therefore obliged to spend the night at an inn. " That " he says " is what they call a really enjoyable day." He thought fox-hunting very dangerous, and was amazed to see women riding to hounds. " It gives me no pleasure to see it " he declares " but they jump like men and are always the first over." He notices that the farmers joined in the national sport. " If they are rich " he says, " and many of them are, they keep two or three hunters, which are not used for anything else." Some who could not afford this expense went out with the harriers, and the country gentlemen hunted with these once or twice a week. " Shooting " de la Rochefoucauld tells us " is not so widely indulged in . . . there is no great quantity of game even here though Suffolk has more game than other counties." He noticed that " the dogs were all pointers ", there was no retrieving. Game preserving on any large scale had not come in, nor was there any driving of birds or wholesale shooting. De la Rochefoucauld found women joining in this sport, and he tells us that many of them were very good shots. He finds that, contrary to the custom in France, there was a close season when game could not be shot, that walking over sown fields was absolutely forbidden, and that anyone who broke down fences had to pay for them in full. Possibly, though de la Rochefoucauld does not say so, this joining of the different classes in various sports, and the strict enforcement of a tenant's claim for damages, may have contributed to internal peace and to there being no revolution in England as there was in France.

The sport of the day being over the company assembled for the four o'clock dinner. There is no mention of luncheon, which if it were eaten at all was a mere snack.

" At four o'clock precisely " de la Rochefoucauld says " you must present yourself in the drawing room with a great deal more ceremony than we are accustomed to in France. This sudden change of social manners is quite astonishing and I was deeply struck by it. In the morning you come down in riding-boots and a shabby coat, you sit where you like, you behave as if you were by yourself, no one takes any notice of you, and it is all extremely comfortable. But in the evening, unless you have just arrived, you must be well washed and well groomed. The standard of politeness is uncomfortably high—strangers go first into the dining room and sit near the hostess and are served in seniority in accordance with a rigid etiquette. In fact for the first few days I was tempted to think that it was done for a joke." "Dinner" de la Rochefoucauld found "one of the most wearisome of English experiences". It lasted for four or five hours, and unlike some of his countrymen who complained that they did not get enough to eat, de la Rochefoucauld was surfeited with food. His host pressed it upon him, inquiring anxiously if he liked it, and "out of pure politeness" he did nothing but eat from the time when he sat down to table until he got up again. The dishes consisted of various meats boiled and roasted, weighing about twenty or thirty pounds. Sauce, de la Rochefoucauld declared, was unknown and ragoûts were seldom seen. "After the sweets" he says "you are given water in small bowls of very clear glass in order to rinse out your mouth—a custom which strikes me as very unfortunate. The more fashionable folk do not rinse out their mouths; but that seems to me worse; for, if you use the water to wash your hands, it becomes dirty and quite disgusting."

The cloth having been removed the table was covered with all kinds of wine, "for" we are told "even gentlemen of modest means, always keep a large stock of wine". On the middle of the table there was a small quantity of fruit, a few biscuits and some butter—a meagre dessert, it would seem; but probably after such a gargantuan meal, the company could not have faced any more. The ladies retired when they had drunk one or two glasses of wine, "and then" we are told "real enjoyment begins—there is not an Englishman who is not supremely happy at this moment". Everyone had to drink in turn as the bottle went round the table and there were numerous toasts. De la Rochefoucauld liked the conversation which followed, politics were discussed and everyone talked with absolute freedom, sometimes he admits that this freedom became indecent. " Complete licence " he says " is allowed, and I have come to the conclusion that the English do not associate the same ideas with certain words that we do. Very often I have heard things mentioned in good society which would be in the grossest taste in France."

He much admires the finely polished mahogany tables, seats, doors and hand-rails. He did not see them in such profusion in France. " I am inclined to think " he says " that the English must be richer than we are ; certainly I have observed not only that everything costs twice as much here as in France, but that the English seize every opportunity to use the things which are expensive in themselves. At all events their tables are made of most beautiful wood and always have a brilliant polish like that of the finest glass."

Mme de Bocage also admired our mahogany. She describes how she dined at a country house near Stowe.

" Immediately after the pudding is despatched " she says " they drink warm punch. After the dessert, especially in the country, the cloth is taken away and the women retire. The table is of fine Indian wood and very smooth, little round vessels, called sliders, which are of the same wood, serve to hold the bottles, and the guests can put them round as they think proper. The name of each different sort of wine is graved upon a plate of silver fastened to the neck of the flask : the guests choose the liquor to which they give preference and drink it with as serious an air as if they were doing penance, at the same time drinking the healths of eminent persons and fashionable beauties. This they call toasting."

Many foreigners speak of the kindness they received at the hands of the country gentry. Macky tells us that he was " unmercifully caressed and entertained by the gentlemen of Dorset after being jeered at in the street and called " Frenchie, Frenchie ". De la Rochefoucauld was astonished at the kindness he received from all the gentlemen around Bury St. Edmunds. " They invited us to dinner and supper " he says ; " we used to stay on at after dinner parties with people who treated us as friends, who would speak very slowly so that we might understand them better, would try, sometimes, to mix a French word or two with their English and would take all possible trouble to give us pleasure."

Of Lord Cornwallis, who commanded the English troops so disastrously in the war with America and who lived at Culford Hall near Bury St. Edmunds, he says, " His kindness to us was something quite out of the common. He had given orders to his gardener, at the beginning of spring, to bring us fruit from his garden up to the time when, as he said, we should come and eat it in his own house. We had the benefit of this order for quite a long time. He is simple in his manner and has no trace of pomposity. We were always exceedingly well treated by him."

Holkham in Norfolk attracted many who wanted to study English farming. Here Thomas Coke, the great agriculturist, held his annual sheep-shearing, " Coke's Clippings " as they were called locally. Among the crowds of Englishmen who attended these gatherings and who were hospitably entertained by the great landowner, there were usually some foreigners. These meetings were started in 1778 and were an annual event through the century. It was not only to the sheep-shearing that foreigners came. Throughout the year Coke would receive letters from agriculturists from the Continent and even from as far as America, asking for permission to see his estates. Dr. Rigby of Norwich, a friend and admirer of Coke, wrote a book entitled

"Holkham and its Agriculture", which was translated into German, French and Italian.

Andrew Jackson, when he was President of America, wrote to Coke, whom he knew well by repute, asking him to receive a fellow countryman, Mr. Bradford, who was himself an agriculturist and speaks of " the high regard which, in this country, is entertained for your character, sentiments and pursuits. Your name " he continued " has reached us under these circumstances which have rendered it dear to your own countrymen and revered in other countries."

Rufus King, the second minister sent to England after America obtained her independence, wrote a similar letter asking Coke to receive one of his countrymen. Later King himself paid several visits to Holkham.

Another guest was William Caton, a Baltimore merchant. He was followed by his son-in-law, Mr. Patterson. It was the custom at Holkham, as it later became the custom in most English households, to have family prayers. For these the company adjourned, after dinner, to the chapel. They were accommodated in a large gallery, while their numerous servants occupied the main body of the chapel. One or two footmen were, however, kept in attendance in the gallery to assist such gentlemen who had drunk so much of Coke's good port that they found a difficulty in rising from their knees. Whether Patterson thought such behaviour unedifying or whether, unlike most Americans of his time, he disliked family worship, we do not know. He, however, declined to attend: " I thank you " he said, " I thank you; but I pray devoutly and sincerely once a week."

Caton wrote grateful letters to Holkham, thanking Coke for his hospitality and expressing the wish to serve him in any way possible. Another guest went further and when he returned to America entrusted to Rush, the

Drawn by Elizabeth Blackwell   *Engraved by R. Havell & Son*

HOLKHAM HALL, NORFOLK

American minister to St. James's, two cases of "American pure beef" as "a tribute of the high respect" in which he held his former host. Owing, however, to the warm weather and a long voyage, the American "pure beef" became so impure that Rush had to dump it in the sea.

Occasionally foreigners would remain in England to study agriculture. There was a young German who was living near Holkham learning to farm. Dr. Rigby, riding round the country with this youth, had been admiring the wonderfully clean state of the land. Although it was a wet season there was not a weed to be seen. Suddenly he espied a piece of charlock, and he pointed this out to the German. The lad leapt from his horse and dragged out the offending weed by the roots, throwing it from him with much indignation. Such, even in those days, was Teutonic thoroughness. John Brunkner, a Dutchman, who studied agriculture and wrote at least one book on that subject, lived for many years in Norwich and probably visited Coke and attended his famous sheep-shearings.

Foreigners criticized and abused many of our customs and institutions, but they had nothing but praise for our agriculture. Zetzner, travelling from London to Bristol early in the century when farming had not reached the great excellence and prosperity which it afterwards attained, is loud in his praises. "It was during this journey" he says " that I saw what a splendid and fertile country this kingdom is . . . agriculture could not be in a more flourishing condition. I saw sheep as big as calves in Germany, sleeping out in the fields, for there is not a single wolf in the whole of England."

The last wolf had been killed in the reign of Charles II, and Zetzner was travelling through some of the most fertile districts of England. He was, however, writing at a time when very little land had been enclosed. The plough-land of each village was divided into strips banked into high ridges so that the furrows between them might carry off some of the rain-water. These strips were so narrow that it was difficult to turn the plough and some were worked entirely by hand. The villagers who owned these strips had not the space or the money to experiment with the new crops of turnips and potatoes which a few of the larger land owners were beginning to grow. The meadow lands, " ings " as they were often called, were common to the whole parish. Everyone had the right to graze a certain number of beasts upon them and frequently they were very much over-stocked. The hay which was grown on these meadows was generally a poor, sparse crop, there were no roots or cake for winter feed, and in the autumn most of the bullocks and sheep were killed and salted down for food. The sheep which impressed Zetzner by their size were in reality very poor and small. Later in the century men like Coke of Holkham and the breeder Robert Bakewell did much to improve the strain both of cattle and sheep, and the enclosures, though they deprived the poor man of his land, and drove him to day labour or the workhouse, enabled the country gentleman and the large farmer to effect great improvements. We can only conclude from Zetzner's description of English agriculture that conditions in Germany were far worse. England had been spared the horror of invasion. There had, it is true, been the Civil War, but that had not lasted long nor been attended with the destruction and miseries of continental warfare.

De Saussure, writing of a later period, remarks on the great prosperity of the farmers. " Some of the farmers of Kent " he says " give their daughters, when they marry, doweries of three or four thousand pounds sterling." He says that their houses were clean and well furnished and that their food was good and abundant. They never ate black bread like the French farmers, and even possessed silver spoons and mugs. Sophie de la Roche met a young Sussex farmer who had actually travelled as far as Rotterdam to see the Kermis, a lengthy and expensive journey in those days.

Sophie tells us that good agricultural land near Colchester was worth twenty-five guineas an acre and a cow fetched as much as seven guineas. She remarks that the farmer's talk was never servile or cringing. " You feel " she says " that they live at their ease and in abundance, and that they dwell under the happy English dominion."

Mme de Bocage tells us how she visited farm-houses and labourer's cottages which were well furnished. She noticed that the poorest country girls drank tea, wore chintz bodices, straw hats and scarlet cloaks. She saw sheep and cattle lying comfortably in the fields with no fear of the wolves which still marauded parts of the French countryside.

De la Rochefoucauld was much interested in agriculture and he stayed for a considerable time in Suffolk. Here he met Arthur Young whom he much admired as an agriculturist, though he found his predilection for carrots, both as a dish and a subject for conversation, rather trying. His house was to be avoided as " his table is the worst and dirtiest and his wife looks exactly like a devil ". English farmers, de la Rochefoucauld thought, had great advantages, for one thing there were no wolves in the country. From the way in which French travellers harp upon the absence of wolves one concludes that they were a serious menace in eighteenth-century France.

De la Rochefoucauld met two farmers who were returning from a riding tour through some of the best cultivated parts of England. They had been to visit other farmers in order to acquire a greater knowledge of agriculture. He describes them as well mounted, and says that most of them hunted with the harriers three or four times a week. "Their houses" he tells us "are always clean and well kept; their barns are in excellent condition, and they are always careful to keep one small sitting room spotlessly clean and sometimes even elegant." At one of these farm-houses he was most hospitably entertained. "The farmer" he says "received us with the greatest courtesy and later we were served with dinner, and we sat to table as calmly as if we had previously had the farmer's acquaintance. Mr. Case's appearance is that of a country-man pure and simple. He has an affable bearing, his manners are polished in the English sense, that is to say without undue formalities, and all the better for that . . . the farm buildings are well supplied with stables, barns and so forth. The barns are full of corn and, in addition, one sees grouped all round the house stacks of peas and barley larger and taller than the house. The farm covers 1,600 acres of land surrounding the house and all linked up together. Mr. Case employs fourteen servants and twelve labourers the year round, and also eighty team horses, he keeps a thousand sheep and a hundred and fifty pigs, fed principally on peas. The harvest lasts for five weeks, during which he employs sixty-three labourers to whom he gives something between forty-two and forty-five shillings as well as food, which costs a prodigious amount. The harvesters have meat three times a day and strong beer in proportion, as well as all the small beer they desire. They consume so much that Mr. Case told us he is obliged to kill two bullocks a week, and three sheep a day."

De la Rochefoucauld describes most of the English villages which he saw as being clean and having "an appearance of cosiness in which ours in France are lacking". He was, of course, in a part of England where agriculture, under good landlords, had made enormous progress, though even here he admits that there were badly built, dirty villages. He thinks that the wages paid to agricultural labourers in England were enormous and as compared with those in France perhaps they were. The English farm worker earned about five or six shillings a week in the county of Suffolk where de la Rochefoucauld was then staying. He says that they did not do nearly as much work as the French, though he admits that Englishmen who had travelled in France disagreed with him, and he might have added that there were Frenchmen who did not share this view.

" The Annual income of a great many commoners in England" Voltaire says " amounts to two hundred thousand livres, and yet these do not think it beneath them to plough the lands which enrich them, and on which they enjoy their liberty." He was probably thinking of some large landowner like Coke of Holkham later in the century, who put on a smock frock and worked in his fields beside his own labourers. That any rich man of good family in France should do such a thing would have been thought utterly incredible and preposterous!

Meister tells us that in 1792 the general cultivation of the country had much improved. One year's harvest, he says, was sufficient to last for fourteen months. " The pasturage is rich, potatoes are superior to any grown in France, and hops are very good; but grapes and all fruits and pulse which owe their perfection to the general influence of a warm sun are not to be had." He was, of course, speaking generally. Grapes, apricots and peaches were grown by country gentlemen and by market gardeners near London. Meister could have bought what he pleased, in season, at Covent Garden. Though he praises the fertility of the English countryside, he also comments on the prevalence of commons and heaths, producing nothing but poor grass where sheep were pastured. In some parts of the country he finds farm and small manor houses uninhabited and falling into decay. He says that they belonged to rich farmers " who would not put themselves to the expense of keeping up houses which were not their own ". In this he shows his ignorance of English country life. No tenant farmer repaired his own house, and few rich landlords in those piping days of English farming suffered their property to fall into decay. The houses which Meister saw probably belonged to small gentry or yeoman farmers, who were being squeezed out by the great rise in prices and the consequent enhanced cost of living.

The beauty of the English countryside was often commented on in an age when natural scenery was not always admired. Pastor Moritz was thrown into " a sort of enthusiastic and pleasing reverie " by the beauty of Windsor Forest and as he travelled, often on foot, he greatly admired " the hedges which in England, more than in any other country, form the boundaries of the green cornfields and give the whole of the distant country the appearance of a large majestic garden ". Moritz was in England in 1782, by which date much of the country had been enclosed by hedges. He continues to rhapsodize and declares that " any of the least beautiful of these views, which I have seen in England, would anywhere in Germany be deemed a paradise ". Moritz lived before the romantic revival, when undulating country, well-farmed land, and pastures, dotted with sheep and cattle, were more admired than crags and torrents, mountains and forests.

He also speaks with approbation of some labourers'

red brick cottages, which he compared favourably with " the mean cottages of our peasants ", and Meister noted the tidy appearance of the villages and that the shops were well furnished with goods. To our modern ideas, the cottages of eighteenth-century labourers were very mean indeed. They were generally built of wood, cob or clay, thatched with reed or straw, and seldom had more than two rooms. Often a working man would build his house with his own hands, there were no byelaws to prevent him. The red brick cottages, which Moritz describes, were to be found on the estates of large landowners who took a pride in their property. It is probable that he had seen some of these, and with the fatal habit, common to many travellers, argued from the particular to the general, ignoring the many thoroughly bad dwellings which dotted the countryside and assuming that the housing of the working classes in England was excellent. It may even be that conditions in Germany were considerably worse. When de la Rochefoucauld reached England he felt himself " transported into another world. I remarked from the first " he says " that atmosphere of comfort which characterizes the country into which I was entering. I observed that all classes of people—peasants from the neighbouring country, servants even—were well clad and remarkably clean, that the furniture in their houses was all of mahogany even in our inn; that they had plenty of those tables which are so dear in France. I saw many carts drawn by fine horses with good harness, such as would involve an expense which our farmers could not face."

Some travellers visited those English country seats which were shown to tourists; Blenheim was such an attraction that it had been necessary to put up pallisades against the lower windows and station men at every door "to keep people back from crowding in on my Lord Duke". A German traveller who went to see it before it was finished, compared the palace to a theatre and said that the talking and shouting of the eight hundred workmen employed upon it made him think of the Tower of Babel.

England was celebrated for her gardens even on the Continent, and probably possessed more than many countries which were considerably larger. In the seventeenth century the formal gardens of France were much admired and imitated. The genius of Le Notre had its effect on some of the famous gardens of England. By the eighteenth century, however, fashion had changed. " The regular symmetry introduced into this science is at present totally neglected " Grosley tells us, nor does he admire the formal gardens which William III introduced from Holland. He describes the Dutch Garden at Kensington Palace as " dismal as a churchyard ". Other travellers were, however, more appreciative. Von Uffenbach tells us of a garden belonging to " Herr Cox, a rich dealer in flax, about three miles from London. It was " he says " ornamented with all kinds of figures cut in box, of which I have never seen so large a quantity, and of such uncommon height. There were all kinds of animals and men, all greater than life size, and some excellently fashioned ships. One of these figures was talking through a tube, into the other end of which another concealed man was speaking. If one goes past unawares it is extraordinarily startling."

Von Uffenbach also tells us of a tulip tree of great size, which he saw in Lord Peterborough's garden at Millbank. " It was higher than a house and thicker than a man."

He saw in Lord Ranelagh's garden at Chelsea a " cucumber tree, which resembled a lime tree ". He tells us that the bark formed cucumbers, which were used as the stoppers of bottles.

De Saussure also saw a tulip tree at Waltham Abbey, which he describes as being forty feet high, and declared that two men with arms outstretched could hardly clasp the trunk. He comments on the well-kept state of English gardens, though he says that there were few flower beds. It may be that he had only visited those great estates whose gardens are described by Count Kielmansegg and where the flowers were a secondary consideration. "The principal features of all English gardens" he says "are gravel or grass walks between irregular high trees or through wild growth, consisting of all kinds of trees, shrubs and flowers, native and foreign, summer houses, seats and benches of all shapes and forms, placed in high or otherwise convenient places, and heathen temples, ruins, colonnades, hermitages, mosques, etc. An effort is frequently made to bring in a natural water course or, failing that, to dig one out artificially with many windings and turnings, waterfalls and bridges so as to please the eye. Pretty views are the principal aim in a garden here, and an Englishman thinks nothing of a garden without water." This was no doubt one of the romantic gardens of what was known as landscape scenery, which Bridgman, Kent and Capability Brown imposed on the English country magnate. Foreign visitors were much impressed with them. Meister is enthusiastic about the beauties of Stowe, "the noblest and the best planned" of all the gardens he had seen in England. Meister describes the triumphal arches, temples, obelisks and Palladian bridges of various seats, and speaks of "the glory and greatness of Blenheim".

"The longest, largest and highest hedge of holly I ever saw" Macky tells us "is in this garden" (Sir

Charles Hedge's at Richmond) " with several other hedges of evergreens, vistas cut through woods, grottoes with fountains, a fine canal running up from the river. His decoy, which is an oval pond, bricked round and his pretty summer house by it to drink a bottle, his stove houses which are always kept at an equal heat for his citrons and other Indian plants, with a gardener brought from foreign countries to manage them, are very curious and entertaining."

Meister mentions " the subterraneous hot bed which he saw at Nuneham." It appeared to him " a contrivance capable of producing charming effects " and it did produce orange trees and other exotic plants. It would be interesting if he had described it in more detail.

Mme de Bocage speaks of the King's estate at Richmond, which had been laid out " to imitate nature ". Trees had been planted, some growing naturally, others were crooked, or what was even more admired entirely withered away. Even the park had artificial hills surrounded by canals which ran into the Thames or watered a grotto which was adorned with sculpture. " Queen Caroline " Madame de Bocage tells us, " who was a lover of subterraneous caverns, caused one to be constructed in the form of a labyrinth in which narrow, dark and winding alleys conduct the feet of the curious. We there meet with the figures of travellers, who seem to walk trembling all the way towards the entrance to the cavern. A low and Gothic door, filled with hieroglyphics, leads to this awful place, to which you descend by a walk, covered with pebbles, overgrown with moss. The enchanter sits upon a tripod loaded with books of magic and armillary spheres. Anne Boleyn and Queen Elizabeth consult him, accompanied by their nurses, persons very proper to assist at these puerile mysteries."

Mme de Bocage comments on the fashionable gardening craze of the moment when she speaks of crooked and withered trees, paths that twisted and meandered and artificial streams in serpentine form. De la Rochefoucauld, with the Frenchman's concern for good food, notices the kitchen gardens. "The English" he says "do not eat half as many vegetables as we do. Consequently their kitchen gardens are quite small in comparison with ours; even those belonging to the largest houses cover only four or five acres . . . generally speaking whatever knowledge they have of the cultivation of kitchen and fruit gardens comes from France."

There were, of course, some travellers who found themselves, for one reason or another, living in the country and were intolerably bored by it. Baretti was one of these, when he was staying at Stansted with Barwell, a rich nabob who had made a great fortune in India by very doubtful means. Men of his sort would often buy a place and set up as country gentlemen to the mingled wrath and amusement of their neighbours. Baretti writes as follows: "I get up at regular hours, am shaved, combed and powdered. Then comes breakfast, followed by a short walk and a little reading to prevent myself from being bored, then dinner and the usual long drinking; then another walk, then tea, then picquet or whist, then supper, after which we go to bed. A very dull life you will say and so do I, and I would gladly change it for another if I could do as I liked; but who can do as he likes in this world? Personally I never could, because I have never found myself rich enough." Baretti was unfortunate in his host. There were men in the country who lived a reasonable and cultivated life. This nabob does not seem to have even cared about sport or concerned himself with parish affairs, or been on the bench.

The weather both in town and country is the subject of much blame and some praise. The fogs both in London and the provinces were more than many foreigners could stand. In the chapter on London we have mentioned the black fogs. Lichtenberg complains of having to light a candle at 10.30 a.m. " One certainly could not endure it " he says " were it not for the other consolations which far outweigh all that. In a word if it were not for the inconceivably lovely naïve creatures ready to be helpful on all occasions, who warm their beds I would wager that all Englishmen would quit England at least for the winter." He would have lost his wager. Setting aside the " lovely naïve creatures ", how many Englishmen would have left the homes of their fathers, draughty and cold though they might have been, the hunting and shooting, justices' meetings, county society, the conviviality of the tavern, club or coffee-house, for the doubtful advantages of foreign travel ? Very few.

The east wind was another trial to foreigners. Voltaire tells us of a young girl, beautiful and rich, who was driven to suicide by the east wind. He also declared that it cast a gloom over the English court and that no one asked a favour of the sovereign except when the wind was in the south or west. " I have never felt such cold " says de la Rochefoucauld, speaking of the hard winter of 1784. " It lasted for nearly four months, during the whole of which the ground was covered with snow about two feet deep and the frost made it as hard as the ground itself. Many of the evergreen trees were completely frozen and the snow which settled on the branches of the fir trees, of which there are large numbers, caused the trees to split in half. . . . My own experience leads me to conclude that the climate of England is very rainy and that it is both colder and windier than that of France. This, however, is contrary to the opinion of a large number of people who hold that, generally speaking, there is little or no difference between the two."

CHAPTER II

Religion, Morals

MONTESQUIEU, after a visit to England in 1736, declared, "Je passe en France pour avoir peu de religion, en Angleterre pour en avoir trop."
In a Protestant country the outward observance of religion is less marked than in a Catholic and possibly had Montesquieu come to England twenty years earlier he might have had a different opinion. In Queen Anne's reign there was marked religious activity. The Society for Promoting Christian Knowledge and the Society for the Propagation of the Gospel which had been founded in the previous reign were both very active. There were societies for the suppression of vice, the reform of morals, and for encouraging Christian faith and the leading of a godly life. Daily services and frequent celebrations of the Holy Communion were advocated in print and pulpit and in the larger towns were often adopted. Sermons, provided they were good, would hold an audience attentive for an hour or two and printed in book form they were eagerly read. Sterne declared that he made more money from his sermons than he got from the sale of the *Sentimental Journey*. Queen Anne had, no doubt, an influence on her reign. The influence of the sovereign was in those days very considerable and, though she may not have had great sense or intellect, she was a good woman and devoted to the church. She bestowed upon the clergy the first

ST. MARY'S IN THE STRAND, 1753

Drawn and engraved by G. Maurer

fruits and tenths which Henry VIII, at the Reformation, took away from the Pope and appropriated. The moral and religious societies, of which we have spoken, had even some effect on the legislature. Magistrates were often coerced into reviving almost obsolete statutes against incontinence, swearing, Sunday trading or travel. Some justices, indeed, refused to receive the evidence tendered them by informers from these societies. Informers have always been disliked, one was even murdered by the mob, and magistrates may have had an uneasy feeling that their own lives would not have satisfied the society for the Suppression of Vice. The zeal for religion and morality unfortunately did not last. Queen Anne died, the first two Georges and their courts had an evil influence upon society, Convocation had been suppressed owing to an unfortunate wrangle between the Upper and Lower Houses. The Bishops and clergy had now no rallying point, no meeting-place where they could discuss matters of importance and encourage each other in a religious life. Men were made bishops rather for their political opinions than for their piety and learning. The clergy were miserably underpaid. Queen Anne's Bounty amounted to only £17,000 a year, which, even in those days, was not sufficient to augment the stipends of all the poorer clergy. Many of them eeked out their miserable incomes as best they could. Some farmed their glebes, some, who were scholarly men, took pupils, others engaged in trade. Macky tells us that " the parsons at Bristol talked of nothing but trade and how to turn the penny ".

" The English clergy, and I fear still more particularly those who live in London " Moritz declares " are noticibly and lamentably conspicuous by a very free, secular and irregular way of life. Since my residence in England one has fought a duel in Hyde Park and shot his antagonist." The jury in this case, in spite of the judge's summing up, brought in a verdict of manslaughter, and the accused, pleading Benefit of Clergy, was merely burnt in the hand by a cold iron. Benefit of Clergy was originally instituted in the twelfth century and by it anyone in orders, who was convicted of a crime punishable with death, could be tried in the ecclesiastical courts, where a lesser penalty would be imposed. When the authority of the ecclesiastical courts was much curtailed the ordinary courts retained the practice. Very heinous offences such as murder could not claim Benefit of Clergy and if the jury in this case had brought in a verdict of murder the duellist would have been hanged. Juries, however, in those days of barbarous punishments, tended to be lenient, and a duellist, provided he fought fairly, was generally sure of sympathy. It was certainly unusual for clergy to fight duels, indeed they were protected by their " cloth ", and public opinion would not have altogether approved of their fighting. There was, however, one clergyman who fought three duels and afterwards became a dean, and the man Allen, of whom Moritz speaks, was never censured by his bishop. Voltaire, commenting on the clergy, says, " A Church of England minister appears as another Cato in the presence of a juvenile or undergraduate, who bawls for a whole morning in the divinity schools and hums a song in chorus with ladies in the evening."

Moritz gives a pleasing picture of the village church at Nettlebed. " I cannot well express " he says " how affecting and edifying it seemed to me to hear this whole orderly and decent congregation in this small country church joining together with vocal and instrumental music in praise of their Maker." He goes on to say that the music affected him even to tears, and that the sermon lasted for only half an hour. After the service he went out into the churchyard where he found the following inscription on a tombstone which had been erected to a parishioner who was a blacksmith:

>My sledge and anvil lie declined
>My bellows too have lost their wind
>My fire's extinct my forge decayed
>My coals are spent, my iron's gone
>My nails are drove, my work is done.

These rhyming inscriptions were very common in the eighteenth century and many are in existence at the present day. There were men who composed them and who supplied many parishes in the neighbourhood, which may account for the similarities we often find. Meister, after visiting Quaker and Methodist services and the chapel of the Spanish Ambassador, goes to an ordinary parish church where he was "much edified by a discourse full of sound doctrine and the sublimest tenets of religion. I was greatly affected" he says "by the exemplary modesty and piety of the preacher's deportment, and the respectful silence and attention of the congregation." Another traveller comments on the simplicity of the sermon. "Discourses" he says "aiming at the pathetic and accompanied by violent gestures would excite laughter in an English congregation. For as they are fond of inflated language and the most impressioned eloquence on the stage, so in the pulpit they affect the most unornamental simplicity." "The English clergy" Voltaire says "have retained a great number of the Romish ceremonies and especially that of receiving, with a most scrupulous attention, their tithes. They also have the pious ambition to aim at superiority. Moreover they inspire very religiously their flock with a holy zeal against Dissenters of all denominations."

He considered that the morals of the English clergy

were better than those of the French. " All the clergy " he says " (a very few excepted) are educated in the universities of Oxford or Cambridge far from the depravity and corruption which reign in the capital. They are not called to dignities till very late, at a time of life when men are sensible of no other passion but avarice."

He noticed that in England it was not possible for a young man of dissolute habits to be raised to the highest dignities of the Church by the intrigues of a courtesan and to continue to conduct himself with no attention to morals or decency. When he tells the English clergy that such a state of things exists in France, " They bless God for their being Protestants. But these " Voltaire adds " are shameless heretics, who deserve to be blown hence through the flames to old Nick, as Rabelais says, and for this reason I don't trouble myself about them."

We may judge from these extracts, as well as from the literature and letters of the eighteenth century that the Church of England had its careless, worldly congregations and ministers and its good devout men who served God with a quiet, simple piety. To say that the eighteenth-century Church was utterly slothful and had no religious sense is to disregard history.

There were no doubt many aspects of religion in England that would not have appealed to foreigners and certainly not to Catholics. De Saussure went to a Presbyterian service. " These ministers " he says " are not permitted either to learn their sermons by heart, or even to write them out or prepare them . . . they preach through their noses in the peculiar manner that the English call cant . . . they scarcely ever smile, they cannot tolerate a jest or a joke and they are so easily scandalized and altogether so very saintly that you cannot refrain from wondering whether it is entirely sincere." The extreme rigidity of the nonconformists was in some measure no doubt a protest against the laxity and worldliness of the established church. A traveller from Germany describes a Methodist service which he attended at the Countess of Huntingdon's Chapel at Bath. He tells us that it was "a little church with benches and slightly raised places for the clergy and singers. The sexes sit apart from each other. On Sunday I attended one of their meetings to which one is admitted by ticket and listened awhile to their psalm singing, but did not stay long. As far as I could judge the service is monotonous though there is a good deal of ranting too."

Lady Huntingdon had been much impressed by the teaching of John Wesley. She was, however, a woman of strong originality and she afterwards quarrelled with her mentor, broke away from him and from the Church of England to which he belonged. She set up a training college for her ministers and there were chapels of her denomination in many parts of England. The most celebrated was the chapel in Spa Fields in London and many members of the aristocracy and some distinguished men occasionally attended it. At her house in Chelsea, Chesterfield, Bolingbroke, Selwyn and Chatham would come and listen to Calvinistic doctrine; some of them even supported the sect with handsome donations.

The religious body which inspired foreigners with the most respect and even veneration was the Society of Friends. After having supper with Lettsom, the celebrated doctor who was a member of that Society, Faujas de St. Fond tells us that "During the remainder of the night I meditated how I should become a Quaker, for if happiness exists anywhere on earth it certainly dwells among these worthy people. . . . I love the Quakers, they inspire me with involuntary veneration."

He goes on to tell us that "all Quakers are merchants", which as he had just had supper with Lettsom he should have known was inaccurate. It was quite true that members of the Society engaged in trade. The Test and Corporation Acts debarred them from many other occupations. De Saussure goes on to say that the Friends "never charge more for their goods than they are worth. Many youthful Quakers" he continues "whose fathers have died leaving them rich, have a longing to wear buttons on their sleeves and live after the fashion of other young men."

The Quakers, their years of persecution and of initial extravagance being over, had settled down to a middle-class respectability. They were looked up to by their fellow countrymen for their honesty and the goodness and charity of their lives. They were a small exclusive body and they did not seek to make converts; but their influence was great. Even Voltaire was attracted by them. No doubt, as de Saussure says, some of their young men rebelled against the strictness of the sect, and their numbers began to decline.

If religion was losing its hold on the people there was one particular in which it was strictly observed. This was the keeping of Sunday. Von Uffenbach remarks with his usual bitterness that this keeping of Sunday was "the only point in which one sees that the English profess to be Christians". His landlady had refused to allow some foreigners, staying in her house, to play the viol de gamba or the flute on a Sunday. She would have been liable to be fined for Sabbath breaking and there were plenty of informers looking out for the reward which was given to such people. Pastor Moritz astonished his landlady's young son by whistling a lively tune on a Sunday morning. This extreme rigour as regards the first day of the week seems to have been entirely a

British characteristic and most foreigners commented on it with much bitterness. It is true that Sophie de la Roche writes of the delightful quiet and peace of the day; but Sophie would praise everything English. Other foreigners were far from complimentary and speak of the horrors of Sunday with much feeling. " On that day " Grosley says " the theatres and all houses of entertainment are shut. All forms of gaming and dancing are forbid. People are neither allowed to sing at home or play upon any instrument. The newspapers, the favourite food of national curiosity, are discontinued, the watermen cease to ply upon the River Thames, the tolls to be paid upon coming into London are doubled and some of them even trebled . . . except in Church time the inhabitants of London wait with their arms across till service is again celebrated or until the day is over without having any other amusement but to gaze in melancholy mood at those who pass to and fro in the streets ".

Sunday was not observed with such extreme rigour by some of the rich or by what would have been known in those days as " the lower orders ". George III rebuked the Archbishop of Canterbury for holding card parties on a Sunday and Count Kielmansegg tells us how he went to court on a Sunday during the reign of George II, dined with Lady Yarmouth, the King's mistress, and in the evening attended a reception at the Princess Severin's.

" Even cards " von Uffenbach tells us " are so expressly forbid that none but persons of quality and those we call genteel play on that day. The rest of the nation go either to church, to the tavern or to see their mistresses."

Moritz describes how the working people of London rose early and, after church on a Sunday morning, went out into the country. The metropolis, though it housed a great number of persons in its congested streets, was then so small that the country could be reached in a half-hour's walk or less from any part of it. Some of these people may have gone to church as Moritz suggests; but a very large portion of the poor knew nothing of religion and never entered a church except for a funeral or a wedding. They wandered out to the taverns and ale-houses in the suburbs of London, and indulged in such sports as cock-fighting, bear- and bull-baiting or prize-fights. Amusements were forbidden on a Sunday; but they were held secretly with the fear of an informer always hanging over them.

The ignorance and vice of many of the working classes had moved the consciences of religious people. In the reign of Queen Anne and to a less extent during the later part of the century, charity schools had been founded, the S.P.C.K. had endeavoured to reach such of them who could read, Wesley's missions had converted thousands; but still there remained a very large number who were quite untouched by religion.

The tolerance of the English in matters of religion is noted by some foreigners, though when we remember the Gordon Riots and other demonstrations against Catholics and Jews, the brutal attacks upon Wesley and his followers and the extreme bigotry of some English clerics, the virtue of tolerance may not seem very conspicuous. Here again it is a matter of comparison; the Inquisition still survived in Spain, and in France the Church did not tolerate Protestants. De la Rochefoucauld, speaking of the English Catholics, says, " The Catholics are wholly undisturbed, in spite of the severity of the laws against them." An informer might, as he explains, go to a magistrate and report that he had seen a certain person at a Catholic service, or that a priest had said Mass. The Justice, however, who loathed informers and probably had Catholic friends, would ask him if he could swear that the prayers were Catholic prayers, was he sure that the priest was actually eating and drinking the sacred bread and wine. "In fact" de la Rochefoucauld says "he put so many questions, demanding so much detail of explanation, that the informer is barely able to answer them and is dismissed without having made good his case". "The Church of England" Grosley says "baptizes all that offer, marries all, buries all, somewhat dearly indeed, but without disturbing the public tranquility by impertinent inquiries." He also noted how men of all sects met together in assemblies and learned societies. One traveller remarks with surprise and approbation that there was no ghetto in London and that Jews did not have to wear any special dress or badge; but Moritz says that the prejudice against Jews was more pronounced in England than in Germany. This, in the light of recent events, strikes us as curious. The Jews were allowed to worship in their synagogues without any interference from the law and the wealthy among them enjoyed a certain amount of protection, at least in the City of London. The English mob were, however, quite capable of setting upon the poor Jews as they walked about the streets on their lawful occasions and they would sometimes wreck Jewish shops. The prejudice may have been more racial than religious. The Jews had returned to England only during the Commonwealth. They had and largely maintained their own customs and even languages and were looked upon as foreigners. In 1753 a bill was passed to naturalize the Jews, but it was repealed the next year in deference to popular outcry. The prejudice against the Chosen People was very strong and has unhappily lasted to the present day.

Of the morals of Englishmen there are varying

accounts. They depended naturally upon the kind of Englishmen with whom the foreigner mixed. He was generally impressed by the honesty of the English merchant, he praised the generosity and charity of the people. In another chapter we have mentioned the large sums of money which were given and bequeathed to the poor. De la Rochefoucauld tells us how the new St. Paul's Cathedral was rebuilt by voluntary subscriptions. " In this way " he says " not only was sufficient money raised, but in the end there was a surplus fund available—a fact which reflects great honour upon the English nation and would not, I fear, have happened in France."

The freedom and independence of the populace is much commented upon by foreigners. " I had not walked " Meister says " fifty yards on English ground before I thought I felt sensations of freedom and the dignity of human nature rising in my breast which I had never experienced before, not even on that day when I trampled upon the ruins of the Bastile."

On the other hand de Saussure tells us that " an immeasurable number of Englishmen are still more corrupt in their morals than in their religion. Debauch runs riot with an unblushing countenance." The English, he says, were " mighty swearers " and he is shocked to see clergymen drinking and smoking in eating-houses and taverns. The English clergy have never been a caste apart as in Catholic countries, but have generally mixed with the people on terms of equality, sometimes indeed and in the eighteenth century particularly, on too gross an equality.

Alfieri was so much pleased with " the beauty of the country, the unaffected morality of the inhabitants, the charm and modesty of the females and above all with the freedom of thought and action everywhere apparent," that he was " almost inclined to forgive the fickleness of the climate and the melancholy which it engendered ". The extreme melancholy of the English is constantly harped upon by foreigners. According to them they frequently lived in a state of unmitigated gloom and depression and often ended in suicide. Grosley declares that this was caused by eating too much beef and drinking vast quantities of beer, which must, he says, " give rise to chyle, whose viscous heaviness can transmit naught but bilious melancholy juices to the brain. If they would drink wine the English would grow more tractable, more gay and less speculative." If gaiety may be acquired by eating little meat and drinking little beer, we ought certainly at the present time to be a very gay nation, though possibly the high price of wine prevents complete ecstasy. Grosley, though admitting that after being in the company of English men of all ranks, conditions and stations and " having experienced in all the same indulgence, the same complaisance, the same kindness ", speaks of the melancholy which characterized them and " which in France is seen only on the countenances of those who have just buried their dearest friends ".

Another traveller tells us that there were people whose families had not laughed for three generations. This extreme gravity is not borne out by eighteenth-century novelists. Fielding and Smollett give us pictures of coarseness and brutality, but their characters are never melancholy. Sterne and Richardson, though they may be accused of sentimentality, are never depressing. It is true that Englishmen did not talk much among themselves and still less with foreigners, they did not embrace each other after the manner of Frenchmen and Germans, and this may have given rise to an idea that they were melancholy. When Mme Vigée le Brun stayed at Knole the Duchess of Dorset told her as they sat down to dinner, " You will find it very dull for we never speak at table." English funeral customs, moreover, may have suggested a general depression and there were many funerals in eighteenth-century England with its high death-rate. Meister considers that these customs were a sign of religious feeling. " As there is here " he says " a greater degree of religious respect and regard shown to young children when newly born, so likewise is there for deceased persons in their departure from this life, and these are both of them convincing proofs of the morality of a people. From the highest to the lowest classes no funeral is conducted without a degree of solemnity. The dead are kept longer above ground here than in any other country in Europe. It is seldom that they are buried before the third day." This was an understatement, the body was usually kept for a week or more before interment, as the fear of being buried alive had come down from the days of the plague when hasty funerals were necessary. The fashion of lying in state was not confined to the rich and great. Except in the case of the very poor the corpse was dressed in its best clothes, the face painted by an undertaker and, in this condition, it was visited by streams of friends and acquaintances and even by total strangers, actuated, some by the wish to pay tribute to a friend or neighbour and many by a gruesome curiosity. Meister goes on to describe the funeral procession, how the hearse had its plumes of ostrich feathers and was preceded by men dressed in black with black bands and scarves. In the case of the unmarried, he tells us, the scarves and plumes were of white. " The burial places " he goes on to say " are preserved in neat order and some of them form pleasant walks where serious persons may indulge themselves in reflections and sentiments of religion and piety."

De Saussure sums up the English character in these words: "My opinion on the whole of Englishmen is that among them you find more sensible, thoughtful, trustworthy and noble-hearted men than in any other nation; but on the other hand a great number of them are whimsical, capricious, surly and changeable."

Baretti had called London "a sink of vice" and a later writer has described it as "the wickedest city in the world because the largest". Both may be true comment; it is difficult to compare degrees of wickedness. Was London worse than Paris or Vienna or Rome? There is no doubt, however, that crime very much increased during the century. Religion and morality declined, the poor became poorer, the enclosures threw the countryman out of work and often drove him to the slums and rookeries of London. In 1753 a gang of criminals terrorized the City of London by their robberies and violence, and officers of justice told Fielding that they had often passed offenders in the street, and though they had warrants in their pockets for their arrest, dared not apprehend them. Penalties increased and at the end of the century there were two hundred offences on the statute book which were punishable with death. The barbarity of the English penal code struck many foreigners with surprise and horror. They declared that it exceeded in rigour anything to be found in France, Italy or the German states. It had certainly no effect in diminishing crime, which became far worse and more widespread as the century advanced and penalties increased.

CHAPTER 12

The Foreigner in Social Life

THOUGH the majority of Englishmen might be cold and distant or even antagonistic to foreigners, men of the higher classes were generally glad to welcome them if they came with properly accredited introductions. They had themselves very often made the Grand Tour and been received and entertained by foreign nobility. Even when war was raging with France men of this class kept up a correspondence with the Continent. Often they had some debt to repay, some hospitality to return. De Saussure tells us of an Englishman who had been stranded in Switzerland without any money. A native of the country lent him sufficient for his needs. Years afterwards this Swiss gentleman visited England and, walking in the Mall, met the man whom he had benefited. He was immediately taken back to the Englishman's house to dinner. Afterwards he was presented by his host with what the latter called "a small present". This turned out to be a deed of gift making the Swiss traveller the owner of a pretty cottage and a small domain near London, which was worth about thirty pounds a year. De Saussure also tells another, and a horrid, story of base ingratitude shown by an English nobleman to a Swiss who had befriended him abroad. "The English" he says "push their virtues and vices further than other people."

De Saussure went to court in 1725 and saw three ladies

presented to the King, " who kissed them all affectionately on the lips, and I remarked that he seemed to take most pleasure in kissing the prettiest of the three. Let not this mode of greeting scandalize you, it is the custom of the country and many ladies would be displeased should you fail to salute them thus." It was a custom which was dying out in the higher classes, the King excepted, though among the middle classes and in the country it lingered. De Saussure says that " the King looked amiable, but those who do not like him say he is not generous in money matters ".

De Saussure was also present on the King's birthday when the City of London presented him with a nosegay according to their usual custom. This was given to the King by " the oldest male inhabitant who could be found, provided he had his faculties and was able to walk ". The King inquired who this strong, soldierly old man was, and what was his age. " Sure, sir," the old man said, " I do not know my age; but I began to carry arms in the Civil Wars under Charles I." The King gave the old man thirty guineas and told him that he should be admitted to Chelsea Hospital with the rank of sergeant.

Lichtenberg " was alone with the King and Queen in an exquisite little room, the Queen being covered with jewels, and the King majestic beyond description in an embroidered costume with his order over his coat ". Lichtenberg, it would seem, was dazzled by the splendour of the royal attire for none of his subjects ever called George III majestic. They called him Farmer George and often sneered at the plainness of his dress and the homely domesticity of his life.

On another occasion Lichtenberg visited Queen Charlotte and found her, as he says, " en famille ". " This morning after nine o'clock " he tells us " I again had to wait on the Queen, who was in cap and black gown." He comments on the beauty of the royal children. Prince Adolphus asked for a stick " but pranced about so terribly among the cups " that he had to be restrained. He observes that he had had more opportunities of seeing the King and Queen " as scarce any other German could boast of ".

Germans generally did not receive that warm welcome from George III which his predecessors had bestowed upon them. George told his people that he gloried in the name of Briton, and he regarded foreigners in the mass with much the same distrust and suspicion as did his subjects. In spite of this Count Kielmansegg tells us that many foreigners were attracted to England by the King's coronation. He and his brother were present, as his aunt had married Lord Howe; but we gather from his account that many others came who had no connection with the English court.

Zetzner was lost and nearly suffocated in the crowd when he watched the funeral procession of William III going from Kensington to Westminster and he saw Queen Anne's coronation.

Towards the close of the century George III became unpopular. Prices were rising, wages for the most part were stationary, the war with America was condemned by most of the business men in the country. According to Grosley, when he came to London some years earlier, the mob was already asking awkward questions. " Why should we bow to George ? " say the insolent rabble. " He should bow to us, he lives at our expense." " They " (the mob) Casanova tells us " hoot the King and the Royal Family when they appear in public and the consequence is that they are never seen save on great occasions when order is kept by hundreds of constables." So little indeed was the King in evidence that de la

Rochefoucauld said that the little tower where the Crown Jewels were kept in the Tower of London was " the only thing in London which shows that a King exists."

Meister, on the other hand, heard " God save the King " continually called for at Sadler's Wells after George III's recovery, and said that he " saw nothing in ancient or modern history comparable to the British Constitution ". A wave of sympathy for the poor King had spread over the country and people were also asking themselves whether they might not be worse off under ' Prinny ' than under Farmer George. The fable of King Log and King Stork was sometimes quoted. When Meister visited England again in 1791, he found a different state of things. The war with France and the consequent increase of taxation was causing much poverty and unemployment. " The words Church and King, which they had rendered sacred " Meister says " are now connected with the word taxes. Those horrid words ' No King, no Parliament ' have been found written in large characters on the walls."

Meister was not much impressed by Windsor Castle. He said that the furniture was " for the most part old-fashioned, worn out and in bad taste " though he admired the pictures and Raphael's cartoons. Moritz described St. James's Palace as " the meanest public building in London." The Queen's Palace or Buckingham House, as it was sometimes called, was then a beautiful building of mellowed red brick. George IV was responsible for the greater part of the present erection. Perhaps he would have agreed with Moritz that " the old palace very much resembled a private house ", which is what it had been before George III bought it for the Queen.

Baretti expressed surprise that English noblemen

should be well mannered and cultivated and compared them favourably in these respects with the Italian nobility. Though he was a man of letters he mixed, as all distinguished literary men could, in what would have been called good society. He thus describes a day as he spent it in England. " I generally get up at eight, when I am shaved and powdered. After drinking tea with a friend, I sit down at my desk and write as I will till three or four in the afternoon. Then I either dine alone with a friend, often with other people, who come in about that time, or else I dine out. About six o'clock I drink tea again, always at somebody else's house and in the company of clever, beautiful women and girls. Then I play at quadrille the whole evening every day, supping where I have been spending the evening, after which we drink tea and chatter till past eleven. The houses I frequent are numerous and would be more numerous did I wish it. My familiarity with English ways and my Italian gaiety which is usually, I might almost say always, greater here than in Italy makes people readily open their doors to me. Blessed England! Rascals are as plentiful here as they are in any other country; but good people abound here in a proportion about thirty times as great as in other countries."

Baretti is almost the only traveller in England who contrived to be gay. Most of them seem to have been oppressed by our climate, our fogs and what they considered to be the coldness and melancholy of the nation.

Mme de Bocage went to a breakfast party at the house of Lady Montagu, as she calls her. She is probably referring to Mrs. Montagu, the celebrated " Blue stocking ". A breakfast party may sound odd in these days; but it was then a very general entertainment, especially among literary people, and the custom lingered on until the introduction of hot lunches in the following century.

Drawn by Canaletti

Engraved by N. Parr

THE ROTUNDA, RANELAGH GARDENS, 1794

ENTERTAINMENTS

"We breakfasted today at Lady Montagu's" she says "in a closet lined with a painted paper of Pekin and furnished with the choicest movables of China. A long table covered with the finest linen presented to the view a hundred glittering cups which contained coffee, chocolate, biscuits, buttered toast and exquisite tea. You must understand that there is no good tea to be had anywhere but in London. The mistress, who deserved to be served at the table of the gods, poured it out herself (this is the custom) and in order to conform to it, the dress of English ladies which suits exactly to their stature, the white apron and the pretty straw hat become them with the greatest propriety."

Count Kielmansegg went to a party at Syon House. "It would not be easy" he says "to imagine a more splendid sight than this gallery presents when filled with people, all vying with one another in the beauty of their dress."

He also dined with the foreign minister on whose table there was, he declares, a piece of beef weighing 227 lb. De la Rochefoucauld does not much care for the English mode of entertaining. "It is customary" he says, "when one gives a party, to invite the whole town, with the result that the crush is oppressive, and most tiring and wearisome to the hostess: in such assemblies, you may well imagine that there is no great pleasure in conversation." Social gatherings in France were occasions for conversation. This was not so in England except at the houses of a few "blue stockings". If men wanted conversation they went to a club or coffee-house, where the talk could be very good indeed. It would not have occurred to them that the ordinary party was a place where they could converse on sensible subjects or that their wives and daughters could be capable of joining in such talk. In many cases, indeed, they would have been quite incapable of anything of the kind.

Travellers in this country noted with surprise and sometimes annoyance that Englishmen talked of nothing but politics. " You may often see an Englishman " de Saussure says " taking a treaty of peace more to heart than he does his own affairs." " These two parties " he continues, speaking of the Whigs and Tories, " are so opposed to one another that nothing but a real miracle could cause them to become united." If the Tories had their way, he thought, the government would be a despotism and if the Whigs remained in power for long there would be anarchy. Meister was present at an election when a vote of thanks was being returned to the successful candidate who was Beckford's nominee. " If the squire " the speaker said " had sent his great dog to us, we should have chosen him as we have done you." This illustrates the great power in politics of the landed gentry, which was only exceeded by that of the aristocracy. In the country the tenants generally voted for their landlord or his nominee. If they did not, they knew that, in many cases, they might be turned out of their houses or lose their employment. In the towns there were constituencies, Pot Walloper boroughs they were called, where everyone who owned his own front door and a fireplace for cooking had a vote. There were also Scot and Lot boroughs in which every man who had lived there for six months and paid Scot and Lot, that is to say poor rates and church rates, was a voter. These boroughs were usually more independent and only voted for the candidate who bribed them most highly. The strife and argument of political life was often extremely boring to foreigners. Lord Tyrconnel who was educated in France came to London when he was thirty years old. Wherever he went in society he met men and women who talked of nothing but politics. He found this so tedious that he resolved to escape from it for one evening at least, and took some ladies of pleasure to dine at a bagnio. To his disgust he discovered that they would do nothing but talk about a bill which was then before parliament. No doubt they had found such conversation agreeable to many of their clients. Lord Tyrconnel, however, left them in a passion and sailed for France almost immediately.

English politics were too noisy, too intricate and obscure to attract the foreigner who knew little of the country. Baretti, however, after his long residence here protests that he is by no means indifferent to politics whether European or English. In a letter to Lord Charlemont he says, " I must for once and very gravely expostulate with your lordship as to that oblique, but degrading accusation, of my being less than apathetically indifferent about politics. Jesus ! Jesus ! how wrong and unjust these lords are apt to be ! Is such an accusation to be brought against a man, who has, for these four months past, been impairing his eyesight, wearing out his thumbs and exhausting his patience in diligently collating half a dozen editions of Machiavel's works, in order to strike out a new one in three enormous quartos ? Come forth of thy back shop, Tom Davies, bookseller de mios pecados, thou who hast paid me so very few guineas for so great a labour. Come forth to bear witness against this lord, as to how I have been and am still, sunk in the very deepest abyss of politics Machiavellian. Was not Machiavel the identical bell— whether of all and everyone of the political flock, the first, the best, the damnedest of them all ? and how can I be taxed with indifference about politics, who am now invested, by booksellers' authority, with the power of supervising, ushering and kicking the chief code of that science into a new edition, and am actually doing it? However, though a thorough politician, I will be so far honest as to own that there was a time, when I was somewhat tainted with doctrines unsound. For instance, there was a time when my notions of liberty (and liberty is the axis round which all manners of politics turn) when my notion of liberty was, that any native of any land was a freeman, provided he had wherewithal to fill his guts after his own taste together with a tolerable share of prudence.... There was a time, my lord, when I thought that a bastard kind of liberty, that did permit a multitude of Catos, Senecas, and Socrateses to call Johnson an hireling, Warburton an atheist, Burke a Jesuit, Mansfield an ass, Wilkes a saint and Junius the saviour of his country ... a multitude of such erroneous notions I own to have once fostered in a foolish pate. But my long meditations upon Machiavel, together with a careful perusal of Algernon Sidney's works and Molesworth's account of Denmark have turned me into so genuine a liberty-man, that I now think it very pretty to curse a King's mother when dead, after having poured upon her all kinds of abuse when alive. I push even so far the liberality of my new notions, that though I know nothing of my queen, I am vastly pleased when I listen to a ballad, when I go along in which a fair queen is called a damned —— without the least ceremony. Huzza, my boys! Wilkes and Liberty for ever! and a plague upon my former apathy about politics!"

Most foreigners praised the women of England. Baretti speaks of " the charming and modest bearing of endless ladies and girls, and among them hundreds of thousands of perfect beauty ". Lichtenberg declared that he had seen many beautiful women in his travels, but that during the ten days he had been in England he had seen as many as in all the rest of his life put together. According to the description of foreigners all Englishwomen had fair hair, blue eyes and fine natural complexions. This was of course exaggeration as may be seen from a glance at eighteenth-century portraits; but it may be there has been a change of type and that fair hair and blue eyes predominated in those days. Another traveller attributed the whiteness of the Englishwoman's skin to " the inconvenience of a cloudy atmosphere ". Mme de Bocage admired Englishwomen. They might dress like the portraits of her great-grandmother; but she found them " extremely affable and obliging in their behaviour ". Possibly they might not be so polite as the ladies of Paris; but they carried, she thought, politeness to excess. She noticed that old women still went into society " without being afraid of showing their wrinkles ", and that young girls went to balls and parties with their mothers and lived " in much less constraint than young ladies amongst us ". She praised the Duchess of Richmond for having shut herself up for six weeks with her children when they were inoculated against small-pox. Few Frenchwomen of fashion, she thought, " would have had so much maternal tenderness as to deprive themselves of pleasure during six weeks for the good of their families ". De la Rochefoucauld thought that English manners, judged by French standards, were bad. The women in particular seemed " lacking in polite behaviour ". " They never " he says " receive any instruction in the subject and all the young people whom I have met in society in Bury give the impression of being what we should call badly brought up: they hum under their breath, they whistle, they sit down in a large armchair and put their feet on another, they sit on any table in the room and do a thousand other things which would be ridiculous in

France, but are done quite naturally in England." He adds that possibly young people would not be quite " so free and easy in London ".

Baretti was delighted with two girls, Ann and Helen Scott, who in the care of their aunt travelled with him as far as Exeter. To his surprise and pleasure they kissed him farewell. He mentioned this to a correspondent but takes care to explain, as de Saussure had done, that it was " according to the custom in England, where kisses are not looked upon as anything shameful as they are in Italy, when they are given and received publickly and in moderation. The ladies " he continues " are, as a rule, angels incarnate, behaving with more reserve and circumspection than those of Italy." He even goes so far as to " stake the best tooth he has in his head that a woman is, as a rule, superior in courtesy, in good sense and in general information to ten men out of twelve ". " Gentle, frank and artless " is another traveller's description of Englishwomen. Some do not comment so favourably. De Saussure complained that women spent their time eating, walking and going to the theatre and to assemblies, that they did very little needlework and inquired about any suitor whether he were rich. One traveller tells us that " women exercise a power equally despotic over both husbands and lovers ", another says that " Englishmen do not spoil their wives by flattery and attention, generally preferring drinking and gambling to female company ". De la Rochefoucauld, after describing how Englishmen amused themselves, says, " The women lead a more sequestered life: nearly always they are at home with their children and sometimes with a female friend. Thus they spend a great part of the day, while their husbands are sometimes—nay frequently—ruining themselves." He admits, however, that husbands and wives were together at all social functions. "They always give" he says "the appearance of perfect harmony, and the wife, in particular, has an air of contentment which always gives me pleasure." He puts this down to the fact that Englishmen had opportunities of knowing their brides as young girls went into society in England. Most marriages he considers were marriages of affection, the young people did not live with their parents, and for these reasons it would he says "be much more to his taste to have an English wife rather than a French one." On the other hand he thinks that English husbands have a great advantage in being able to divorce their wives for misconduct; though he admits that the process was very costly and difficult.

Sometimes the foreigner made a great impression on the susceptible heart of an Englishwoman. Mrs. Thrale, as we know, consoled herself in indecent haste with the Italian Piozzi, a foreigner, a Papist and public singer as her horrified friends pointed out. Fanny Burney married M. d'Arblay. An unknown lady inserted the following advertisement in the *Public Advertiser* of January 1, 1761. "Whereas a tall young gentleman above the common size, dressed in a yellow, grounded velvet (supposed to be a foreigner) with a solitaire round his neck and a glass in his hand was narrowly observed and much approved of by a certain young lady at the last ridotto. This is to acquaint the said young gentleman, if his heart is entirely disengaged, that if he will apply to A. B. at Garraway's Coffee House in Exchange Alley, he may be directed to have an interview with the said young lady, which may prove greatly to his advantage. Strict secrecy on the gentleman's side will be depended on."

It would be interesting to know whether the tall young gentleman in yellow grounded velvet responded to this invitation and what was the outcome of the interview, but this is one of the tantalizing things we are not told.

Alfieri had an affair with a woman, probably Lady Ligonier, whom he speaks of as Lady L. He used to visit her at her house near Cobham in Surrey, and spent the intervals when he was not in her society in " weeping and raving in his chamber, or in galloping furiously from place to place and leaping over hedges and ditches to the imminent hazard of his neck ". Lord L., who had been apprised by one of his servants of what had taken place, sought for Alfieri and found him in a box at a London theatre. He immediately challenged him to a duel, though seeing that his arm was in a sling, offered to defer the encounter. To this Alfieri would not agree and he and Lord L. went out to the Green Park together. Probably Lord L. had scruples about fighting a disabled man, for he let Alfieri off very lightly with a slight wound. Alfieri took his lady love for a tour through England and would have married her after her divorce if he had not discovered that she had had a previous intrigue with her husband's groom.

In a chapter on social life some mention must be made of clothes and fashions.

Frenchmen did not approve of the way in which Englishwomen dressed. They said that they wore old-fashioned, ill-fitting garments and that they had large feet. They explained that the enormous size of female feet was due to the Englishwoman's passion for taking exercise. Even those of them who were well-to-do and whose husbands kept coaches liked to walk in their gardens and on their estates. This was an extraordinary habit and, of course, quite fatal to feet.

Clothes were dear in England. Baretti, writing to his brother Filippo who was contemplating a journey to England with a friend, advises him to bring what clothes he needs with him. "Don't trouble" he says "to bring more than one trunk between you with a dozen shirts each, a travelling coat and two good coats of smooth cloth without much lace except on the wastecoats, for on these it does not matter if the lace is even rich. If the coats were much laced, you would be obliged to have a carriage, unless you wanted to appear ridiculous. Bring a good supply of silk stockings and scarves, so as not to have to buy them here, where everything costs the eyes of the head, and remember to leave the long tails to your wigs behind you, and the wooden heels to your shoes, if you do not want the English boys to run after you in the street." The wig with tails may have been what Johnson in his dictionary describes as "the bagwig—an ornamental purse of silk tied to men's hair". It was not then the fashion in England, though much worn on the Continent.

Baretti also advises his brother not to bring muffs as he would "only be laughed and jeered at for them". Silk and camlet coats he considers unnecessary even in July and August. "Coats" he says "must either be of cloth or velvet."

Apparently foreigners dressed even more extravagantly than the English. Henry Angelo tells us that "foreigners of every learned or scientific profession practising here, were remarkable for their rich display of costume. Many of my father's friends and acquaintances, whose finances made it expedient for two or three to club expenses for a furnished second floor in the back streets of Soho, yet contrived to pay £30 or 40 for a dress suit, laced ruffles a bag and sword."

They had to be careful, however, what they wore or carried.

"It is the rule of the people of London" Grosley says "not to use or suffer foreigners to use our umbrellas of taffeta or waxed silk." Thomas Hanway, when he returned to London from the Continent in 1750 had met with the same opposition to his umbrella. The hackney coach men strongly protested; they would lose fares, they declared, if this foreign fashion were established and people could protect themselves against the rain. They would no longer hire hackney coaches; it was not to be tolerated. In spite of being hustled and jeered at, Hanway insisted upon carrying his umbrella in the streets of London, and after a time other people followed his example.

Sophie de la Roche complained that " in this land of freedom of thought women may not go out without hats. She tells us " how four ladies entered a box at the Haymarket " where she was " with such wonderfully fantastic caps and hats perched on their heads that they were received by the entire audience with loud derision. Their neckerchiefs were puffed up so high that their noses were scarce visible and their nosegays were like huge shrubs, large enough to conceal a person." A quarter of an hour afterwards four women appeared on the stage, dressed exactly like the ladies in the box and greeted them as their friends. The gentleman who was escorting them was so overwhelmed with embarrassment, that he fled from the place, leaving the ladies to their ordeal. One of them tried to hide her face with her fan, but an actress called to her by name and at last the ladies fled. They were followed by a number of persons from the pit and gallery calling after them in ridicule. This episode illustrates the unthinking cruelty of many of the English when they met with anything which they considered peculiar or outlandish. Sophie says that Englishwomen exaggerated and spoilt French fashions. She also tells us that many of them " neglect their petticoats to a degree which grieved me not a little ".

Grosley declares that English ladies were " so sensible of their beauty that they neglect their dress ".

Apparently Englishwomen came to adapt themselves more nearly to French fashions. Meister tells us that " The dress of their hair and the fashion of their clothes are much improved since 1789. . . . London has the happiness at the present time of being in possession of the united talents of M. Leonard and M. Bertin, not to mention a number of French femmes de chambres . . . as the English ladies are daily improving in taste they should altogether lay aside the use of stays. I mean such as are stiffened and rise high in the neck . . . some ladies, instead of these stays have taken to wearing girdles, very broad and fixed pretty high." The simpler French fashions which came in after the revolution may have been more easily copied than very elaborate styles. These still lingered, however, in the country and among old-fashioned people. Meister tells us how much he disliked " padded ladies ". Lichtenberg mentions the four or five or six ostrich feathers, white, blue, red and black together, which it was then the custom for women to wear on their heads, and which cost the large sum of a guinea each. " They quiver " he tells us " at the slightest movement of the heart—that is to say if the head can be moved by the heart, and are able to express love or hate and quod sic and quod non and heaven knows what. It makes the pretty girls very pretty and the plain ones very plain." De la Rochefoucauld notices with surprise that Englishwomen did not use rouge. There had been a time when it was certainly the fashion, but when he came to England in 1784, it was " a practice which had completely disappeared ".

Mme de Bocage thought that " the white apron and pretty straw-hat which the ladies' wore in the morning became them with the greatest propriety " though they made "a less brilliant appearance in the evening . . . when dressed according to the French fashion. I cannot conceive " she continues " why all Europe should be so complaisant as to adopt our modes, the changes of which the inhabitants of our own provinces cannot possibly conform to, which foreign nations receive very late, and never in the same manner in which they were introduced at Paris. Every country has its peculiar language, manners and ideas, and ought, in consequence, to have its peculiar mode of dressing, which must always suit better to the shape and make of the inhabitants than any borrowed habit." Von Uffenbach was surprised to find ladies at Epsom Races wearing what he thought were men's clothes with feathered hats. These riding habits consisted of coats cut like a man's with waistcoats and sometimes stocks. They were, of course, worn with skirts but even so were looked upon, when they first came in, as very mannish and improper. They were, however, more practical and convenient than hooped skirts and elaborately trimmed bodices and were often worn when walking or travelling.

Foreigners were surprised to find all classes wearing much the same kind of clothes, some might be ragged and dirty, but they still bore resemblance to what had once been the fashion. De Saussure found very few women wearing woollen gowns. Even maidservants wore silk gowns on Sundays and holidays and were almost as well dressed as their mistresses. At one time poor women wore red cloaks, but Moritz, who notes this, assures us that " women in general from the highest to the lowest, wear clothes which differ from each other less in fashion than they do in fineness. Fashion is so generally attended to among the Englishwomen that the poorest of maidservants is careful to be in the fashion. . . . There is through all ranks here not near so great a distinction between high and low as there is in Germany."

De Saussure found a citizen's wife, who in his country would not have dreamed of such ostentation, buying gold brocade cloth which the Princess of Wales had said was too dear for her. She even went to court in a dress made of this sumptuous material. " No Frenchwoman " de Saussure assures us " would have dared venture to pay court in such a fashion."

Moritz notices that farmers, instead of wearing coarse frocks as they did in Germany, " were dressed with some taste in fine cloth no different from townspeople ".

The only people whose dress differed were the Welsh. Macky says that he was " particularly pleased to see the Welsh ladies come to market at Shrewsbury " in their laced hats, their own hair hanging round their shoulders and blue and scarlet cloaks like our Amazons ".

De la Rochefoucauld describes men's dress as being " very simple—black breeches and silk stockings. Such is the correct dress for occasions like these (for balls in the country). In order to be something quite out of the common a man may go on wearing his cravat and his hair in a pigtail with his ordinary clothes. The well dressed men wear a new coat every time, but a plain coat with nothing sumptuous about it." Lichtenberg, who lived also in good society, complains that he was forced to dress twice a day, in different costumes, which was not the custom of his country. He tells us how the housemaid who lighted his fire and put a warming pan in his bed wore a black and white silk hat and " a kind of train ". One would imagine that this was an extraordinarily inconvenient dress for doing house work; but Lichtenberg says that she carried her warming pan " with as much grace as many German ladies would a parasol ". The fact that the English classes dressed so much alike and that there was in England no peasant costume and no wooden shoes greatly impressed the foreigner.

Mme de Bocage says that buildings which were called palaces in London " at Paris would pass only as large houses, which men of fortune amongst us would find many faults with ". Our luxury, she thought, did not equal that of Paris; we had no armchairs and were quite satisfied with common chairs. Our rooms were seldom very large, even in noblemen's houses.

After receiving several presents including some fruit which she " did not know what to make of, being only used to comfits " she says, " so many marks of affection please me the more as the English are thought to be sincere in their affections. They are falsely accused of receiving foreigners ill. I cannot believe that their favours are confined to us. It is true that we but little resemble the natives of our country, who dislike any opinion that is not familiar to them." She goes on to praise the public spirit of the English and notes how Gresham had built the Royal Exchange at his own expense and Dr. Harvey, who had discovered or rediscovered the circulation of the blood, bequeathed his estate to the faculty of medicine. Sir Hugh Middleton had diverted the course of the New River to supply part of London with water, and Sir John Cotton had left his valuable library to the nation. " There is nothing " she says " which should more excite our wonder."

It is pleasant to know that one foreigner who had spent many years in England and sampled its merits and its vices wrote the following farewell.

" Farewell beautiful England; farewell home of virtue, farewell sink of vice. . . . Willingly do I forget all the sufferings I have endured in thee for so many years; but I shall not forget the great kindness thou hast shown me, nor shall I ever cease to remember with gratitude all thy honoured sons who have helped and encouraged me in my hour of need." This encomium was written by Baretti at a time when he was leaving the country and felt tender towards it. On another occasion he writes with less enthusiasm. The English he says " are by no means altogether bad ", and goes on to praise their courage and generosity.

In a chapter on English social life something must be said about the servants who were the prop and stay of all upper and middle-class families. On the whole it was thought that the English did not make good servants. They were more independent than their brethren on the Continent. If a master struck his servant, the man would be very likely to knock him down. Maidservants could see no reason why they should not dress as well as their mistresses and have similar amusements. Voltaire was surprised to see servants at Greenwich Fair elegantly dressed and riding on horseback. He took them at first for " people of fashion ".

Foreigners considered that servants' wages were very high. Grosley speaks of " a fat Welsh girl who could scarce understand English, and could only wash and scrub and sweep ". He does not say how much more she might be expected to do ; but he thinks that her wage of six guineas a year with a guinea tea money was enormous. Cooks, he tells us, got the huge sum of twenty guineas a year. These would, of course, have been very good cooks ; but some travellers after eating our meals, declared that there were no good cooks in England. What worried foreigners more than the high wages, which they did not usually have to pay, were the tips or vails as they were called.

" If you take a meal with a person of rank " de Saussure tells us " you must give every one of the five or six footmen a coin on leaving. They will be ranged in a file in the hall, and the least you can give them is a shilling each, and should you fail to do this you will be treated insolently the next time."

It was said that footman's vails doubled their wages, and that Sir Robert Walpole's porter got eighty pounds in Christmas boxes. If porters were not remembered on this handsome scale their masters were never at home.

This imposition was hard on foreigners who were often poor men and who did not tip so highly in their own countries. "In truth, my lord, I am not rich enough to take soup with you often" was the reply one traveller gave to an invitation.

The English themselves deplored this system of vail giving, and recognized that it was hard on foreigners. There was a suggestion which came, it was said, from Scotland, that all vails should be abolished. A few hosts tried to adopt this, they raised their servants' wages and implored their guests not to give vails. Suggestions from Scotland, and the desires of English gentlemen, were, however, quite unavailing. The vail has remained with us under its present trivial name and will most probably always continue.

LEICESTER SQUARE

CHAPTER 13

Foreign Quacks and Impostors

THE eighteenth century was still an age of superstition. True, a small number of enlightened men laughed at it, and in 1736 witchcraft ceased to be a capital offence. Among the populace, however, the belief in witchcraft and a hundred other superstitions still flourished. Astrological almanacs and charms were sold by the thousand, every sort of fortune-teller, necromancer, quack and adventurer set up in business and generally did very well. That England was a happy hunting ground for such people gradually became known on the Continent and a stream of adventurers came over. There was the French astrologer who was consulted by George I and who told him that he would not live for more than a year after the death of his wife. At the end of this period the King left England to die in his beloved Hanover. He took a sad farewell of his court, and assured them, with tears in his eyes, that he would never see them again. To many of his subjects this did not seem to be a matter for tears, and they were both surprised and annoyed when he came back again in rude health. In July 1776 the Italian swindler Guiseppe Balsamo, who had assumed the high sounding name and title of Count Alessandro di Medina Cagliostro, came to London. He was accompanied by his wife and a secretary and brought with him three thousand pounds in gold, besides money and jewels. He set up in rooms in Whitcomb Street near Pall Mall as a professor of the occult sciences and an infallible guide to lucky numbers in lotteries. He also had a scheme for weaving silk out of hemp, and what made him really famous and sought after, his physical regeneration. This was a course which would cure all ills or nearly all and indefinitely prolong life. It consisted of a forty days' course of baths, sweating, starvation, medicines, purgatives and a diet of roots. Many people came to him and declared they were cured. Possibly they were; starvation and roots after a long course of over-eating and drinking may well have had an excellent effect. Then Cagliostro did an unwise thing, he started what may be called a mumbo-jumbo of " Egyptian Masonry ". This naturally aroused the suspicions of English Masons and people began to whisper that he was an impostor who had swindled many people on the Continent. He contrived, however, to make friends with Lord George Gordon, who, however mad he may have been, was not a knave; other acquaintances were less reputable, a man and his wife of the name of Fry and an Italian called Vitellini set out to swindle him. They actually contrived to extract from him half his gains, and not content with this had him arrested for a fictitious debt of one hundred and ninety pounds and subsequently on a charge of witchcraft. Cagliostro was acquitted on both these charges; but was imprisoned at the King's Bench at the instance of a fellow countryman, Badioli, who had become one of his sureties. Lorenza, his wife, now took a hand. She went to mass one Sunday at the chapel of the Bavarian minister, and here by her sighs and tears attracted the attention of a member of the congregation, Sir Edward Hales. He gave her money and afterwards, when her husband was released from prison, employed him to do mural paintings at Hales Place. Cagliostro knew nothing of art and his effort only excited derision. Then he took to lecturing and as popular lecturers must hold their audiences, his lectures took a sensational turn. He stated in one of them that the people of Medina, whose country was infested with wild beasts, were in the habit of fattening their pigs with arsenic. They then turned them out on the countryside to be devoured by ferocious animals. These promptly died of arsenic poisoning; but why the pigs had not died of it Cagliostro did not explain. That anyone should have troubled to refute such nonsense seems odd; but a certain M. de Morande, the editor of a French newspaper, expressed grave doubts about the authenticity of these curious facts. Cagliostro promptly sent a letter to the *Public Advertiser* inviting de Morande to breakfast with him. The principal diet at this meal was to be a sucking pig fattened according to the Medina custom.

" The day after our breakfast " Cagliostro wrote " one or more of four things will happen. Either both of us shall die or we neither of us shall die, or you shall die and I survive, or I shall die and you survive. Of these four chances I give you three, and I bet you 5,000 guineas that on the day after our breakfast you shall die and I shall be perfectly well. You must either accept the challenge or acknowledge that you are an ignorant fellow, and that you have foolishly ridiculed a thing which is out of your knowledge." M. de Morande did not accept the invitation and declared that Cagliostro was " the greatest impostor of the age ". Finding that his many enemies were working against him and that Londoners were becoming less sympathetic, the count spoke mournfully of going to live with the wild beasts of the jungle where he was sure of finding friends, and departed for Paris.

We have mentioned George Psalmanazar in a previous

chapter. His real name is not known, but he was supposed to be a Frenchman. While serving in a regiment abroad he became acquainted with the chaplain, a man called Innes. He was already posing as a native of Formosa and talking some gibberish which he called Japanese. Innes, who was thoroughly disreputable, had discovered that the man was an impostor; but thought that something might be made out of him. He suggested that he should become a convert to Christianity. Psalmanazar agreed, and Innes then wrote to Compton, Bishop of London, informing him of his success in converting this heathen Japanese to the Church of England. The Bishop, without apparently making any inquiries, invited them both to come to London. Psalmanazar accepted with alacrity, he was thankful to get out of the army. Innes had had the bright idea that Psalmanazar should write a History of Formosa. He set to work, and in two months—he had been educated at a Jesuit College—he turned out a book, written in Latin, which purported to be a history of his native island. Innes translated it into English and when they came to England it was sold to a London bookseller. It was full of the wildest absurdities; but as no one had been to Japan it was difficult to refute them. Lord Pembroke, it is true, expressed some doubt whether Psalmanazar's statement that Greek was studied in Formosa could be accurate; but nevertheless the book achieved great success. He next turned his attention to the Church Catechism which he translated into what he called Japanese. There could not, one supposes, have been any large sale for this in England; but the book undoubtedly brought him prestige among the clergy and religious people. Innes, who perhaps realized that doubts were being expressed about his accomplice and that the imposture might not go undetected, went off to

Portugal to be Chaplain-General of the English troops there. It was a post he had obtained through the good offices of the Bishop of London. Psalmanazar was now without his mentor and he did a very foolish thing. About a year before he had met Halley, who was then Savillian Professor of Mathematics at Oxford and afterwards became Astronomer Royal. Halley made some awkward inquiries about the position of the midday sun in Formosa and also how long the twilight lasted. Psalmanazar's answers were most unsatisfactory. If he had been wise he would have kept very quiet about the matter; but in his preface to the new edition of his book on Formosa he stated that Halley and his friends had been completely satisfied with his replies to their questions. This was too much for the future Astronomer Royal. The man who predicted the return of a comet, who discovered the proper motions of the stars and the long inequality of Jupiter and Saturn, might be expected to know something about the position of the midday sun in Formosa. He declared indignantly that Psalmanazar's answers to his questions had been anything but satisfactory, and that he was a rank impostor. Psalmanazar, finding that deceit no longer paid, took to hack writing for the booksellers. He also produced his own memoirs in which he confessed that " out of Europe I was not born, educated nor ever travelled ", and he expressed deep sorrow " for the base and shameful imposture of passing upon the world for a native of Formosa and a convert to Christianity, and backing it with a fictitious account of that island, and of my own travels, conversion etc. all or most of it hatched in my own brain without regard to truth or honesty ". Psalmanazar may have been sincere in his protestations of repentance. Mrs. Piozzi tells us that his " pious endurance of a tedious illness ending in an exemplary death confirmed the strong impression which his merit had made on Dr. Johnson ". Boswell mentions him two or three times. He belonged to the club where Johnson met the metaphysical tailor and where he " sought after George Psalmanazar the most. I used to go and sit with him at an ale house in the city " Johnson told his biographer. The latter says that Johnson reverenced Psalmanazar for his piety, and would as soon have thought of contradicting a bishop. There were very, very few people whom the Great Cham would have refrained from contradicting.

Gustavus Katterfelto was another quack. His fellow countryman, Pastor Moritz, declared that "every sensible person considers Katterfelto as a puppy, an ignoramus, a braggadocio and an impostor; notwithstanding which " he adds " he has a number of followers ". For some time he travelled about the country in a caravan accompanied by large black cats. Then he cast his eyes on the metropolis, the Mecca of every great quack. He hired rooms in Piccadilly and inserted the following advertisement in the *Morning Post* of July 31, 1782.

" Wonders, Wonders, Wonders, Wonders! are now to be seen at No. 22 Piccadilly, by Mr. Katterfelto's newly improved and greatly admired solar microscope. Mr. Katterfelto has, by a very long and laborious study, discovered at last such a variety of wonderful experiments in natural and experimental philosophy and mathamaticks as will surprise all the world. Mr. Katterfelto will show the surprising insects on the hedge larger than ever, and those insects which caused the late influenza as large as a bird, and in a drop of water the size of a pin's head, there will be seen above 50,000 insects. N.B. After his evening lecture he will discover all the various arts on dice, cards, billiards and O.E. tables.

KATTERFELTO AND DR. BOISSY

Admittance, front seats 3s. second seats 2s. and back seats 1s. only. Mr. Katterfelto likewise makes and sells Dr. Bato's medicines at 5s. a bottle." This idea that disease could be caused by living organisms was something quite new and it might have startled the medical world had it been advanced by anyone more reputable. Epidemics, it was thought by the older school of physicians, were caused by heat, damp, and other natural causes. It had been the accepted opinion in ancient Greece, and the more conservative among the doctors saw no reason to doubt it. There were, however, some of the younger men who thought that disease was carried by minute particles in the air, which they called formites. They could be, they suggested, destroyed by soap and water, fresh air and various disinfectants. That any of them might be seen under a microscope was never imagined, except by Katterfelto.

Dr. Boissy was another foreign quack who flourished in London. Perhaps it is incorrect to call him a quack, for he certainly gained a reputation and a fortune as a skilful surgeon. His methods of advertising, however, suggested a mountebank rather than a medical man. Accompanied by a servant in livery Dr. Boissy would drive every Thursday to Covent Garden, where under one of the colonnades a platform had been erected. Boissy having climbed up to his post by means of a ladder, would seat himself at a table on which were his medicine chest and surgical instruments. He would then rise, take off his gold-laced cocked hat and bow right and left to the surrounding multitude. On these occasions he never charged his patients any fees. This was the practice of many of these mountebank-physicians. They may have been moved by compassion or have realized that here was a cheap and excellent advertisement. In any case the poor could have paid very little and men like Boissy were making a fine income out of the well-to-do.

Philip Loutherbourg and his wife, who came from Alsace, were pure philanthropists. When people came to them " they looked upon them with an eye of benignity and cured them ". They never charged any fee. Unfortunately the patients were admitted by ticket and there was always a great crowd. Unscrupulous people sold their tickets to those who had been waiting wearily for hours and charged as much as two or three guineas for them. The Loutherbourgs were said to have effected hundreds of cures. They met, however, with great opposition and suffered, they declared, " all the malignity that man could suffer joined to ungrateful behaviour and tumult ". Disgusted at this reception of their kindness they gave up their cures and retired into private life.

Then there was a Mr. Lattese from Piedmont, who declared that by a long course of experiments he had " discovered the wonderful secret of procreating either sex at the joint option of the parents. Should they desire a daughter ", which few people did, " the success cannot be warranted with absolute certainty ; but should they concur in their wishes to have a son, they may rely that by strictly conforming to a few easy and natural directions they will positively have a boy. Mr. Lattese thinks fit to premise that he will pay no attention but to letters post paid and signed with real names, directed to him at the Antigallican Coffee-House by the Royal Exchange." Mr. Lattese did not remain long in business, probably his clients were disappointed with daughters.

These quacks and impostors whom we have mentioned were at the head of their profession, but there were also others, the travelling mountebanks, half entertainers half quack doctors, who set up their booths in the market places of country towns and even penetrated into remote villages. " Please ma'am the mountebanks be come " was the exclamation of a village serving maid on seeing a coach draw up at the door of her mistress's house. The only vehicle of that sort which she had ever seen in those remote parts was the coach which carried the mountebanks. Macky, when he was staying at an inn at Winchester, saw " a coach with six bay horses, a calash and four, a chaise-marine and four enter the inn yard ". He tells us the liveries " were yellow turned up with red, and there were four gentlemen on horseback in blue trimmed with silver. . . . There was no coronet on the coach, but a plain coat of arms with this motto *argento laborat faber*. Upon enquiry I found this great equipage belonged to a mountebank and, that his name being Smith, the motto was a pun upon his name. The footmen in yellow were his tumblers and trumpeters, those in blue his merry-andrew, his apothecary and spokesman. He was dressed in velvet and had in his coach a woman who danced upon the ropes."

These mountebanks were immensely popular, especially in the country. They provided such entertainments as tight-rope dancing, tumbling and various acrobatic feats. They also sold powders, pills and ointments, which they assured their audiences had already cured half the crowned heads of Europe. Some even produced certificates, medals and large seals, which they said had been bestowed upon them by grateful princes.

Carlyle declared that the age of superstition ended with the French Revolution. This was not, however, the opinion of the German traveller Memnich who, describing the England which he saw in 1799, said that it contained quacks and impostors " beyond any other in the whole world ". Mme de Bocage does not go so far as this; but she describes with amazement how ten thousand Londoners ran away out of the city because a soldier had prophesied that it would be entirely destroyed by earthquake on a certain date. " Such a prediction " she says " would never have occasioned so much terror in Paris."

In the country, especially in remote places, every kind of superstition flourished. Baretti says that at Honiton he was shown the stool used for ducking witches. This was in 1760, and such a method of dealing with witches had for many years been illegal. It still lingered, however, in out-of-the-way places, and the belief in sorcery had lasted through the eighteenth century and into the present day.

BIBLIOGRAPHY AND INDEX

BIBLIOGRAPHY

COUNT FREDERICK KIELMANSEGG. *Diary of a Journey to England.*
J. MACKY. *A Journey through England in Familiar Letters.*
J. B. S. MAYOR. *Cambridge under Queen Anne.*
HENRY MEISTER. *Letters written during a residence in England, 1799.*
CESAR DE SAUSSURE. *A Foreign View of England in the Reigns of George I and George II.* Translated by Mme Van Muyden.
Z. C. VON UFFENBACH. *London in 1710.* Translated by W. H. Quarrell and W. C. J. Quarrell.
VOLTAIRE. *Letters concerning the English Nation.*
G. BARETTI. *A Journey from London to Geneva through England.*
H. DE. MISSON. *Memoires et Observations faites par un voyageur en Angleterre.*
G. C. LICHTENBERG. *Briefe aus England.*
J. E. ZETZNER. *Londres et Angleterre, A.D. 1700.*
ARTHUR YOUNG. *Travels in England.*
J. W. ARCHENHOLZ. *A Picture of England.*
DEFOE. *Tour through Great Britain.*
MALET. *Annals of the Road.*
THOMAS BURKE. *The English Inn.*
A. W. M. STIRLING. *Coke of Norfolk and his friends.*
RIGBY. *Holkham, its Agriculture, etc.*
MME DE BOCAGE. *Letters concerning England.*
VITA SACKVILLE-WEST. *Knole and the Sackvilles.*
L. COLLINSON MORLEY. *Guiseppe Baretti and his friends.*
F. DE LA ROCHEFOUCAULD. *A Frenchman in England.* Translated by S. C. Roberts.
CHARLES HARPER. *Stage Coach and Mail.*
PASTOR MORITZ. *Travels in England.*
M. GROSLEY. *A Tour of England.* Translated by T. Nugent.
A. BARBEAU. *Life and Letters at Bath in the 18th Century.*
FAUJAS DE S. FOND. *A Journey through England and Scotland.* Translated by Sir Archibald Geikie.
G. M. TREVELYAN. *English Social History.*
BOSWELL'S *Life of Johnson.*
J. H. CAMPE. *Reise Durch England.*
ELIE DE BEAUMONT. *Un voyageur français en Angleterre en 1764.*
SOPHIE DE LA ROCHE. *Sophie in London.* Translated and edited by Clare Williams.
G. J. CASANOVA DE SEIGNALT. *Mémoires.*
PSALMANAZAR, GEORGE. *Memoirs.*

INDEX

Abershaw, Johnnie, 36
Addison, Joseph, 78–9, 105, 107, 116
Alfieri, Count Vittorio, 28, 33, 164, 180
Angelo, Henry, 181
Anne, Queen, 154–5
Astley, Philip, 88

Bacchelli, Giannetta, 108
Bach, Johann Christian, 109
Bakewell, Robert, 142
Balsamo, Guiseppe, 189
Baretti, Guiseppe, 58, 63–4, 90, 92–3, 106, 109–10, 113–14, 119, 120, 151, 167, 171–2, 175–6, 178, 180–1, 187, 198
Barry, Mrs., 81
Barwell, Mr., 151
Baskerville, Mrs., 103
Bath, 14–15, 116, 125–9, 159
Beauclerk, Topham, 63
Beaumont, Elie de, 97
Beckford, William, 174
Bedlam, 118–19
Bentley, Richard, 96
Birmingham, 14, 103, 121, 123
Blenheim Palace, 147, 149
Bocage, Mme de, 2–3, 83–4, 98, 105, 108, 110, 138, 143, 150, 172, 177, 183, 186, 197–8
Boissy, Dr., 195–6
Boswell, James, 17, 194
Bridewell, 74
Brighton, 1–2, 34
Bristol, 15, 120, 129, 155
British Museum, 69–70
Brunkner, John, 141

Buckingham Palace, 171
Buggiani, Signor, 108
Buononcini, Giovanni, 109
Burmann, Pieter, 132
Burney, Fanny, 179
Bury St. Edmunds, 139, 177
Buxton, 132

Cagliostro, Count, 189–91
Cambridge, 47, 97, 106–7; University, 95–9
Campe, J. H., 123
Canterbury, 49
Caroline, Queen, 150
Carter, Elizabeth, 19
Casanova, Giovanni Jacopo, 4, 28, 37, 76, 78, 84, 87–8, 103, 170
Case, Mr., 144
Caton, William, 140
Charles III, King of Spain, 25
Charlotte, Queen, 169–70
Chelsea, 148, 159
Cheltenham, 129
Christ's Hospital, 100–1
Coke, Thomas, 139–42, 145
Colchester, 20, 120, 143
Compton, Bishop of London, 192–3
Coram, Captain Thomas, 116
Cornelys, Mrs., 84
Cornwallis, 1st Marquis, 139
Cotton, Sir John, 186
Cowper, William, 14
Cuper's Gardens, 85

Defoe, Daniel, 44, 47
Devon, 26, 28

INDEX

Dimsdale, Baron, 70
Dorchester, 28
Dorset, Duchess of, 166
Dorset, Duke of, 108
Dover, 1-2, 22, 28, 33, 43
Duval, Claude, 34, 36

Edinburgh, 14
Elizabeth, Queen, 72
Epsom, 130; Races, 184
Eton, 101
Euston, 135
Exeter, 13, 19, 26, 36

Fielding, Sir John, 34, 63, 113, 165, 167
Flamsteed, John, 92
Foundling Hospital, 116-17
Fours, Miss, 107
Franklin, Benjamin, 49, 92, 104, 115
Friends, Society of, 159-60
Frome, 121

Gabrielli, Dido, 107
Gammon, Richard, 13
Garrick, David, 63, 76-8, 80-1
George I, King, x, 189
George II, King, 150, 169
George III, King, 129, 161, 169-171
George IV, King, 171
George, Prince, of Denmark, 25-6
Godalming, 20, 25
Grafton, Duke of, 135
Greenwich Fair, 187; Hospital, 117-18
Grosley, M., 7, 22, 28, 31-3, 40, 43, 46-7, 53, 58, 60, 63-4, 66, 78, 82, 94-5, 102, 112, 114, 148, 161, 163, 165, 170, 181, 183, 187
Guildford, 26, 32

Hales, Sir Edward, 190
Halifax, 120

Halley, Edmund, 193
Hampstead, 131-2
Handel, George Frederick, 107-109, 117
Hanway, Thomas, 182
Harrogate, 132
Harrow, 101
Harvey, Dr. W., 186
Harwich, 2-3, 28, 40, 103
Hedge, Sir Charles, 150
Hervey, Sir Augustus, 37
Hogarth, William, 112, 117
Holberg, Baron, 100
Holkham, 139-41
Honiton, 198
Hounslow Heath, 26
Huguenots, 123
Huntingdon, Countess of, 36, 159

Innes, Mr., 192-3

Jackson, President Andrew, 140
Johnson, Samuel, 17, 63, 106, 194
Jordan, Dorothy, 81

Katterfelto, Gustavus, 194-5
Kensington Palace, 148
Kent, 47, 142
Kielmansegg, Count Frederick, 2, 8, 20, 23, 28, 36, 40, 67, 69, 71, 74, 76, 79, 81-2, 96, 107, 116-18, 128, 149, 161, 170, 173
King, Rufus, 140
Knole, 108, 165-6

Lancashire, 26
Lattese, Mr., 196
Le Blanc, Abbé, 128
Leeds, 120
Leicester, 30
Lettsom, Dr. I., 159
Leverian Museum, 70
Lewes, 26
Lichtenberg, George Christoph,

INDEX

35, 46, 52, 56, 60, 62, 77, 81, 103, 107, 122, 124, 152, 169, 176, 183, 185
Livingston, John, 130
London, 1–7, 8, 23–4, 28, 35–8, 43, 48–54, 55 *et seq.*, 102, 104, 113–18, 152, 155, 161, 167, 181–2
Lord Mayor's Show, 70–2
Loutherbourg, Philip, 196

Macadam, John Loudon, 27
Macky, M., 7, 45, 47, 50–3, 64–5, 73, 78, 98, 115, 125, 127–31, 133, 138, 149, 155, 185, 197
McLean, Captain, 34
Manchester, 21, 23
Margate, 133
Marlborough, Duke of, 76
Marlborough, Sarah Duchess of, 30
Meister, Henry, x, 5–6, 9, 31, 46, 59, 66, 70, 78–9, 81, 87, 99, 111, 112–14, 117, 124, 145, 149–50, 157, 164, 171, 174, 183
Memnich, Herr, 197
Metcalf, John, 31
Middleton, Sir Hugh, 186
Mirabeau, Comte de, 95
Miranda, Francesco, 68
Misson, H. de., 11
Monroe, Dr., 118
Montagu, Elizabeth, 130, 172–3
Montesquieu, Charles Baron de, 154
Morande, M. de, 191
Moritz, Pastor, 2, 5–6, 10, 11–12, 14, 21, 23, 26, 28, 42, 45, 48–9, 58, 61, 66, 70, 79, 83, 93–4, 97–8, 101, 103, 112, 124–5, 146, 155–6, 161, 166, 171, 184–5, 194

Nash, "Beau", 125, 129
Nettlebed, 156
Newbury, 47
Newcastle, 13–14
North, Lord, 35
Northampton, 26
Nuneham, 150

Oldfield, Nance, 80
Oxford, 8, 43, 48; University, 95–100

Palmer, John, 14–15
Paoli, General, 106
Parliament, Houses of, 66–8
Pembroke, Earl of, 30, 37
Petworth, 25
Pickford, M., 23
Piozzi, Gabriel, 106, 179
Portsmouth, 25
Preston, 27
Psalmanazer, George, 100, 102, 106, 191

Radcliffe, Dr., 128
Ranelagh, 82–4
Ranelagh, Viscount, 148
Rann, Jack, 34
Reynolds, Sir Joshua, 63, 110
Richardson, Samuel, 165
Richmond, 35, 132, 150
Richmond, Duchess of, 177
Rigby, Dr., 141
Roche, Sophie de la, xi, 8, 36–7, 43, 57, 60, 69, 80, 88, 94–5, 100, 102–3, 116–18, 123, 143, 161, 182
Rochefoucauld, Duc de la, 32, 53, 59–60, 65, 70, 89–90, 98–9, 134–9, 143–5, 147, 151, 152, 162–4, 171, 173, 177–9, 183, 185
Russell, Dr., 133

St. Fond, Faujas de, 46, 48, 58, 121, 123, 132, 159
St. James's Palace, 171
St. Paul's Cathedral, 66, 164
Salisbury, 30; Cathedral, 124
Salter, William 18

203

INDEX

Saussure, Cesar de, 3–5, 24, 28, 32, 48, 55, 60–2, 66, 68, 71–4, 79, 85–6, 88, 113, 115, 118, 124, 142, 149, 158, 160, 164, 167, 168, 174, 178, 184–5, 187
Severin, Princess, 161
Shaftesbury, 30
Shakespeare, William 78–9, 105, 125
Sharpe, James, 21
Shrewsbury, 21, 185
Siddons, Sarah, 80–1
Sloane, Sir Hans, 93
Spa Fields, 159
Stansted, 151
Stein, Baron von, 121
Sterne, Laurence, 154, 165
Stilton, 47
Stourbridge, 33
Stowe, 138, 149
Stratford-on-Avon, 125
Suffolk, 143–5
Sussex, 26, 47, 143
Swift, Jonathan, 42
Syon House, 173

Telford, Thomas, 27
Thrale, Mrs., 93, 106, 179, 193
Tower of London, 68–9
Tunbridge Wells, 129–30
Turpin, Dick, 34
Tyburn, 64, 74
Tyrconnel, Earl of, 174–5

Uffenbach, Z. C. von, xi, 3, 24, 35, 68, 73, 76, 85–9, 92–3, 96–7, 99, 101, 103, 106–7, 119, 122, 131, 148, 160–1, 184

Vanneschi, Signor, 107
Vauxhall, 82–3
Vigée de Brun, Mme, 165–6
Voltaire, 79–80, 93, 104–5, 112, 124, 145, 152, 156–8, 160, 187

Walpole, Horace, 26, 34, 66, 108
Walpole, Sir Robert, 188
Waltham Abbey, 149
Warner, Richard, 21
Wedgwood, Josiah, 123
Wesley, John, 159, 162
Westminster Abbey, 66, 105
Wigan, 27
Winchester, 197
Windsor, 25, 42; Forest, 146; Castle, 171
Woolman, John, 32
Wren, Sir Christopher, 67

Yarmouth, Countess of, 161
Yarmouth, Great, 1–2, 14, 133
Yorkshire, 29, 120
Young, Arthur, 26–8, 43, 143

Zetzner, Herr J. E., 5–6, 47, 69, 70–1, 77, 80, 94, 141–2, 170